THE DEATH OF CONTRACT

Grant Gilmore, 1969. Photo courtesy of the University of Chicago Law School.

The Death of Contract

Grant Gilmore

Edited and with a Foreword by
Ronald K. L. Collins

Ohio State University Press
Columbus

Original hardcover publication June 28, 1974.

Copyright © 1974, 1995 by the Ohio State University Press.
Foreword copyright © 1995 by Ronald K. L. Collins.
All rights reserved.

Library of Congress Cataloging-in-Publication Data
Gilmore, Grant.
The death of contract / Grant Gilmore : edited and with a foreword by
Ronald K. L. Collins. —2nd ed.
   p.   cm.
Includes bibliographical references and index.
ISBN 0-8142-0676-X (paper :   acid-free)
1. Contracts—United States.   2. Contracts—Philosophy.
I. Title.
KF801.G54   1995
346.73′02—dc20
[347.30662]   95-11979
                                                        CIP
                    ISBN 0-8142-0676-X

Cover design by Donna Hartwick.
Type set in Trump Mediaeval.
Printed by Cushing-Malloy, Inc., Ann Arbor, Michigan.

The paper in this book meets the guidelines for permanence and durability
of the Committee on Production Guidelines for Book Longevity of the Coun-
cil on Library Resources.

                9   8   7   6   5   4   3   2   1

CONTENTS

FOREWORD

Every original book has the
seeds of its own death in it . . . .
—*Oliver Wendell Holmes, Jr.*
(Feb. 1, 1919)

WITHIN THIRTY years of the publication of *The Common Law* (1881), Oliver Wendell Holmes, Jr., feared that his great achievement was "dead."[1] Once an original, it had become a classic. Like Blackstone's *Commentaries* and Kent's *Commentaries* after that, it now belonged to law's history. The magnificent Holmes no longer moved the law—he had already settled his share of it.

In a few but notable ways, something of the same is true of Grant Gilmore and *The Death of Contract*. It too was an original, as much as can be. It too drew considerable attention and provoked investigation, reconsideration, and controversy. It too affected our conceptions of law—the law of

---

To Lloyd James Tevis (1920–90), my contracts teacher.—R.K.L.C.

vii

Contract. But it attempted to move our conceptions far from Holmesian shores. Hence, unlike *The Common Law*, it was *unsettling*.

The Death of Contract was a book for an "age of anxiety."[2] Gilmore's tract[3] seemed rather like the anti-paragon of Contracts. It took a lot of religious-like doctrine out of the law.[4] In fact, that was a real part of its appeal. In this sense, Gilmore's little work is akin to a *Common Law* for postmodern times.

Now, some twenty years after its original publication, *The Death of Contract* may itself appear dead. After all, it is becoming or has become a classic, and there are no classics among the living. So why read such a book? Here are a few (often related) reasons.

The Death of Contract contains some splendid discussions and assessments of contract doctrines, contract restatements of the law, and of course, contract cases. Such considerations point, we are told, to the collapse of the law of contract into the law of torts. All of this is laid out in Gilmore's compact tract, a work that opens with a declaration of death and closes with a reflection on resurrection.

Bear in mind that some of these are *bold* claims. Clearly, there is truth in this telling, but it is nevertheless a story that must be examined. Whether one agrees or disagrees with Gilmore's particular claims is nowhere as important as engaging in the process of critical inquiry. If law is to prove itself, it must be cross-examined. This little book helps to teach its readers, in a variety of ways, something very important about the art of such critical cross-examination.

Part and parcel of the art of legal analysis is the ability to understand how the law is conceptualized and reconceptualized by those who direct its course. Law, like life, is struggle. And Gilmore struggled—as many from Emperor Justinian to Judge Richard Posner have—to influence our notion of law. Each generation of lawyers has its builders and its levelers, its conceptualists and its contextualists, its formalists and its anti-formalists, its Langdells and its Llewellyns, and so on. Witness within the book the spirited tug-and-pull of this struggle; witness as well the battle for your mind. When the final line is past, will you stand conceptually alongside Holmes or Gilmore,[5] or somewhere in between, or somewhere far away?

If indeed "law is the calling of thinkers,"[6] then there is much to be gained by reading (and rereading with care) *The Death of Contract*. For Gilmore projected case and doctrine through his own analytical lens onto the wide screen of jurisprudence for all to examine. It was a lesson in legal *thinking* more than a mere summary of contract law. This lesson is offered, among other places, in the "Origins" chapter of Gilmore's book. For example, how and why is a given legal argument made? What does that argument presuppose? Are there other ways of looking at the same argument? What follows from starting with a given line of argument? To ask these questions is to embark on that analytical process heralded in *The Death of Contract*. It is how one comes to know or doubt the logic of the law.

Furthermore, this slim volume shows that what is grand in the law transcends the law—call it philosophy or philosophy of law. The notion is as old as Plato's *Laws*, though for our modern purposes the point may be more readily grasped by reference (again) to Holmes's *Common Law*. For Holmes, as for Gilmore, the primary task at hand was not legal history or case-law analysis, however important such matters are. The two scholars engaged in more speculative endeavors linked to juristic principles.

In a variety of thought-provoking ways, Gilmore's *Death* may be a philosophical counter to Holmes's *Common Law*, at least as portrayed by Gilmore. Holmes organized history and classified cases; his jurisprudence concerned that "inevitable process of legal development" (p. 46) from one point to another. Gilmore moved in the opposite direction. He questioned Holmesian history, challenged case classification (pp. 18–19, 29–30, 61), and saw disintegration (pp. 110–11) where Holmes saw development. Holmes was a grand-theory man (p. 63), whereas Gilmore was quick to point out that this or that theory was never as grand as it was held out to be (pp. 66, 75, 84, 103–4). Illustrative of this, Part II offers a rather robust "debate" between Holmes and Gilmore over the issue of the character of the law ("objectivist" vs. "subjectivist") and its role in judging the acts of men and women. While this was a conceptual quarrel (between a dead jurist and a lively scholar) over a celebrated contracts case, *Raffles v. Wichelhaus* (1864), it all too readily turned elsewhere—to those larger questions of the kind battled over by the great minds of the ages. Thus, speaking from a "higher jurisprudential level," Gilmore was critical of

Holmes's objectivist take on law and life, dismissing it as the "great metaphysical solvent—the critical test for distinguishing between the false and the true" (p. 47). In sum, *The Death of Contract* invites us to consider Holmesian thought as expressed in *The Common Law*, if only thereafter to rebut it.

> Thought is biographical. For
> behind every great work lies the
> person, in all complexity
> and contradiction.

A few words about the man may help to put his novel work and bold words in more human perspective. Grant Gilmore (1910–82) was a Yale man bred in the Boston suburbs. He had all the ivy-league credentials—A.B. (1931), LL. B. (1942), law journal editor in chief, all stamped with the Yale seal. He also held a Ph.D. in French studies (1936). His Yale doctoral dissertation, *Stéphane Mallarmé: A Biography and an Interpretation*, examined the life and work of the unorthodox nineteenth-century French symbolist poet. At first, Gilmore taught French at Yale University. Several years later he returned to Yale to begin his illustrious career in the law, counseled by a brilliant psychoanalyst—one Helen, his spouse.

Gilmore (the man who distrusted Harvard)[7] received the James Barr Ames Prize, Harvard Law School's coveted award for distinguished work in legal scholarship by individuals not on the Harvard faculty. This was the same award bestowed on Judge Benjamin Cardozo and on Professor Arthur Linton Corbin. The work that won Gilmore the prize was his two-volume, 1,500-page treatise, *Security Interests in Personal Property* (1965), a work dedicated to his mentor Arthur Corbin. Equally impressive, the executors of Oliver Wendell Holmes's papers chose Gilmore (a curious selection) to complete the definitive biography of the eminent jurist. Gilmore was also the scholar who, along with his Yale colleague Charles L. Black, coauthored the highly regarded treatise titled *The Law of Admiralty* (1957). By way of an aside: In 1959 Professor Corbin privately recommended Gilmore to serve as an adviser for the drafting of the *Restatement (Second) of Contracts*. True to fate, the nod never came, and Gilmore never became a "restater."

By many measures, his was an eclectic and impressive vita. Except for Gilmore's self-imposed but generously compensated short exile at the University of Chicago (a place he apparently detested),[8] here was a man who met his moment and was steering fast and far into the future. The next stop in that future was Columbus, Ohio.

In April of 1970 then University of Chicago law professor Grant Gilmore pointed his Saab toward Columbus, where he was to deliver the Law Forum Series Lecture. Though the series was not as renowned as the Storrs Lectures—those would come a few years later upon his return to Yale—the Ohio State Law School program had already attracted more than its share of legal luminaries. The notables included the much-heralded Roger Traynor of the California Supreme Court; Joseph T. Sneed, the respected Stanford law professor and former president of the Association of American Law Schools; and Telford Taylor, the distinguished Columbia University law professor who had earlier served as the chief United States prosecutor at the Nuremberg war crimes trials.

We will turn to Gilmore's famous lectures shortly. Before doing so, a few more things ought to be added to the record in order to complete this little biographical sketch of the man and his work.

After *The Death of Contract* there were more articles and more lectures, the Storrs Lectures on Jurisprudence (1974) being the most important. A few years later those lectures would assume book form in another acclaimed compact work, *The Ages of American Law* (1977). And there was also Gilmore's highly regarded scholarly casebook, *Contracts: Cases and Materials* (the 2nd edition, 1970, with Friedrich Kessler; and the posthumous 3rd edition, 1986, with Kessler and Anthony Kronman).

Late in May of 1982 the then Vermont Law School professor (he returned to Yale in 1973 and left in 1978) offered his last lecture, not in New Haven, but in Hartford, at the University of Connecticut School of Law. It was an inspiring commencement address entitled "What Is a Law School?"[9] A few days afterward, on the day of Benjamin Cardozo's birth, Grant Gilmore, the agnostic, died in his sleep on May

24, 1982. He was seventy-two. Later, in the winter of 1982, a memorial service was held at Yale Law School, with addresses by his friends:

Guido Calabresi: "[Grant's] last works are not of the present."[10]

Anthony Kronman: "Grant was a magician in an age of bureaucrats."[11]

And a little later Gilmore's senior coauthor and his Yale law colleague added his own remembrance for the *Yale Law Journal:*

Friedrich Kessler: "[Grant liked to] strike out boldly . . . in his attempt to blaze new trails."[12]

The New Haven farewell notwithstanding, Grant Gilmore left his papers to the Harvard Law School—the same institution that held firmly to the conviction that "inspiration should be distrusted."[13] Incredible. He was as contrary in death as he had been in life. Then again, perhaps "complicated" is a better word.

By the time he died, the complex and cantankerous Gilmore had made his own peculiar mark on the law, and a stark mark at that. Still, no gravestone marked his memory.

His scattered ashes were his final consideration, illusory as
that may seem.

> The Death of Contract . . . is one of those few books
> that deserve our most careful thought and attention.
>
> —Richard Epstein

Law is inextricably linked to language, typically expressed
in the written word. Hence, careful reading is essential to
law. Constitutions, cases, statutes, and regulations all demand a certain kind of attentive reading[14] if they are to have
any meaning. Gilmore, the Mallarmé-inspired wordsmith
and the UCC Article 9 draftsman, knew this lesson far better than most. In fact, a great deal can be learned about this
larger issue by stepping back and reflecting on how to read
The Death of Contract.

Was Gilmore right about the "origins" of Contract? Was
he right about his assertion that Justice Holmes was the
prime mover in creating the "revolutionary" doctrine of
consideration? Or was he right about the historical background of, say, the old contracts chestnut known as the
Peerless case (pp. 39–45)? What about his take on Hadley v.
Baxendale (pp. 54–59, 92–93), or his notion of "doctrinal disintegration" (pp. 110–11), or his famous claim that the law
of contracts was being absorbed into torts (pp. 95–104)? In
important part, how one answers these questions and there-

after evaluates Gilmore's thought depends, I believe, on how one approaches this provocative little work.

In life and law, certain things need to be taken at face value, provided we understand both the "face" and the "value" before us. Gilmore made striking claims; and the bench, bar, and academy have vigorously responded to them, as the bibliography to this book suggests. There is much in that face–value exchange that has enriched, and continues to enrich, our understanding of law generally and contract law specifically. But there is more to Gilmore than such exchanges. There is a more subtle, even sophisticated, side to *The Death of Contract*.

In *The Death of Contract* Gilmore sometimes wrote for the mind's eye of the "attentive reader" (e.g., p. 78); in other works, he wrote heedful of that same reader, or the "astute reader," or the "careful and determined reader." Once, he openly defended the importance of forms of writing directed to "a hierarchy of readers."[15] This, obviously, was natural to a talented writer of Gilmore's stripe, and especially to anyone who, like himself, had studied the peculiar weave of the poetic webs spun by Mallarmé.

Mindful of these suggestive hints, one may justifiably ask: Is it reasonably possible that *The Death of Contract* had a meaning beyond what was "easily comprehensible," a meaning discernible only by "close and careful study"?[16] Just what is that meaning, and how can one (like a lawyerly Columbus) discover it? The answer, of course, depends on the reader.

One *possibility* is that in writing *The Death of Contract*

Gilmore may have replicated (in part or whole) the very phenomenon he was critiquing. There is irony here, but only to those who can detect it. For Gilmore may have sometimes parodied the case summaries of Dean Christopher Columbus Langdell and Professor Samuel Williston, imitated the elegant lecture style and intellectual craft of Holmes, and spoofed the rest of his inattentive readers. In much the same spirit, for those who wanted certainty, he gave them certainty, albeit in the negative. For those who wanted a tidy explanation of how the world of Contract came into being, he gave them a Genesis. For those who wanted a story of the Decline of Contract, he gave them a "survey of the brief, happy life of the general theory of contract" (p. 93). For those who wanted the bottom line, he gave them Death. For those who wanted hope, he held out Resurrection (p. 112). And so on. It was almost as if Gilmore were warning: "If you take what I say as Gospel, may Fate have mercy on you."

Then again, it is possible that Gilmore was simply wrong and wrongheaded in places, that he took unwarranted liberties with case law and case history. But if Professor Richard Epstein and others are even partially correct in their claim that *The Death of Contract* "is one of those few books that deserve our most careful thought and attention,"[17] then we owe it to this great legal mind to at least consider the possibility that he was doing something other than making obvious mistakes, if any mistakes there were. "Despite the book's many shortcomings," said Gilmore, "I have not been persuaded by my critics that my *reconstruction* was fundamentally in error."[18] What are we to make of this?

> Theory is important. Theory helps us understand our
> world, stimulates additional hypotheses, and offers a
> framework for less theoretical thinking.
> —*Robert A. Hillman*

Indeed, theory *is* important. Grant Gilmore surely knew that. Precisely because he did, he may have felt the need to warn of the dangers of theory, or of grand theories of the kind that had been, and continue to be, so important in steering life and law. Theory can help us understand our world *up to a point.* Theory offers a framework for thinking provided it is never too certain or rigid, and never too "scientific." Speculated Gilmore: "Man's fate will forever elude the attempts of his intellect to understand it. . . . The quest for the laws which will explain the riddle of human behavior leads us not toward the truth but toward the illusion of certainty, which is our curse."[19] Think more, theorize less might have been his maxim.

Was *The Death of Contract*, then, a clarion call for what would become the critical legal studies (CLS) movement? Yes and no. Like the legal realists and the CLS adherents who followed them, Gilmore was quite skeptical of the way in which the law could be manipulated. He railed against "ritual incantation[s]" (p. 49) in the law, those sacred rules which have little or no connection to reality. Put irreverently: Courts avoid practicing on weekdays what they so eloquently preach on Sundays (p. 52). So yes, there was surely a "critical" component in Gilmore's thought.

Gilmore's critical edge did not, however, lead to suicidal

dead ends. As his friend and colleague Ellen Peters noted: "[His] enduring message was that abandonment of the illusion of certainty did not signal nihilism, or anarchy, or anti-intellectualism."[20] Lawyers need to be able to accept, understand, and work with the unruly and uncertain ways of change. Gilmore took Langdell, Williston, and the creators of the *Restatements* to task for failing to appreciate this. By comparison, what Gilmore said of Justice Joseph Story was at least partially applicable to himself: "[He] was an easy-going pragmatist who looked on rules of law not as mystical absolutes but as tentative approximations subject to change as the conditions which called them forth themselves changed."[21] Likewise important, this no-Nietzsche man praised Arthur Corbin as that "non-establishment revolutionary" (p. 66) whose treatise on contracts was the "greatest law book ever written" (pp. 63–64). The revolutionary thought of Yale's Arthur Corbin apparently suited Gilmore; whether the radical and more contemporary thought of Harvard's Duncan Kennedy (a leading voice in the CLS movement) would have won his full approval is far more questionable.

While Gilmore was certainly no feminist,[22] he surely agreed with that tenet of feminist thinking critical of abstract and impersonal values, of universal solutions, of "logical" imperatives. Gilmore, after all, was the one who challenged Langdell's male-like cosmos, mockingly labeling it a universe of "doctrine and nothing but doctrine—pure, absolute, abstract, scientific—a logician's dream of heaven" (p. 107). Though not entirely, logic lives in context, in personal lives. If that proposition can be squared with Gilmore's thought, then his work may well have had something of a feminist quality. But it was not a work premised on gender-related notions of power and principle; it was, at best, a work seemingly adaptable to such notions.

Gilmore long ago noticed the law and economics campaign and hinted that it might one day claim its place in the jurisprudential sun. "Professor Posner," wrote Gilmore, "feels that nineteenth century negligence theory was economically as well as legally sound and that the gradual erosion of the theory in this century is to be deplored. *If he turns his attention to contract, his conclusions will no doubt be the same"* (pp. 163–64, n. 247, emphasis added). As it happened, the professor turned judge did turn his attention (and that of others) to contracts, and the rest of the story may gradually become the status quo in private law. The idea of a rule of law rigidly premised on notions of "allocative efficiency" and rational decision makers smacked of yet another "well-articulated theory," perhaps just that kind of formalist theory "waiting in the wings to summon us back to the paths of . . . discipline [and] order" (p. 112). Posner would assume Langdell's mantle. Perhaps, as suggested by the important last line of *The Death of Contract,* the law and economics movement was one of those "unlikely resurrection[s]" made possible by Fate's "Easter-tide" (p. 112).

Not one to hoist philosophical flags too high or too often, Gilmore believed that "a fondness for unitary theory and universal abstraction has never been the exclusive pos-

session of conservative thinkers."[23] The "new conceptualists," as they were dubbed, were ushering in their own questionable (though "extremely interesting") unitary theories
to challenge the Langdellian and Posnerian theories. Or so
Gilmore thought. Tracking the legal realists, Professor Ian
Macneil (the captain of the new conceptualists) argued in favor of a "relational" theory of contract. The law of contract
could be found not simply at the moment of signing documents but also in the extended future relationships between
the parties. If Gilmore harbored doubts about all of this,[24]
maybe it was because he felt that too many transactions did
not fit the Macneil mold, or perhaps that in many such
transactions old notions of mutual assent still remained
key, still governed, and did so in a way that *resist[ed]* commercial reality."[25] Absent such suggestions, it is somewhat
puzzling that Gilmore took exception to the relational
school of contracts.

On a related front, what would Gilmore have thought of
the budding "transactional law" movement? Like the modern transactionalists, he was skeptical of the "neat and tidy
and all-of-a-piece" world portrayed in casebooks (p. 61). And
he was surely leery of the "deception" and "distortion" (p.
30) seemingly inherent in the case-method approach to legal
education. But unlike the transactionalists, Gilmore (as evidenced by his own casebook) never really abandoned
Langdell's method, his "madness." Apropos of the mixed
message in this irony, he once quipped that "the case-
method has been our shame as well as our glory."[26] He was
so critical of the case method that he could not bring himself

to leave it. Maybe that helps to explain why in his Ohio lectures Gilmore never actually considered the relevance of theory to areas beyond appellate case law. The idea that the law of contract was as much in a transaction as in an appellate case, or that the law's *planning* function was as important as its *adversarial* function, were matters not really pondered in *The Death of Contract*. Whether law's norms "reside" in decisional or transactional constructs, or both, the key question here is, what are the main contractual objectives and how best can they be realized and explained? How a client is counseled, a contract drafted, a deal negotiated, or an agreement performed all depend on the answer to this question. If his slim volume never really answered such questions, it is because Grant Gilmore, like the Langdellians he rebuked, never quite asked them.

Gilmore was no contractual Moralist. He would thus have parted conceptual paths with legal moralists such as Harvard law professor Charles Fried, author of *Contract as Promise* (1981). It is not that Gilmore was an avowed contractual atheist; it was rather that he was suspicious of Absolutes and the unequivocal imperatives they generate (pp. 52, 105–6). The idea that any "promise principle" could be all-purpose, however morally appealing, is a variant on the all-purpose "consideration" theme Gilmore so vigorously challenged (pp. 19–24, 69). Another "ivory tower abstraction" or another "balance-wheel of the great machine" of theory (p. 19) is how Gilmore might have characterized the Fried principle. Admittedly, promise—as in promissory estoppel—assumed the role of a bright star in the Gilmorean universe. But even a bright star does not a galaxy make.

Notwithstanding all that has just been offered, it would be a mistake to assume that Gilmore was pedestrian or mechanical in his approach to law. He certainly was no anti-theory "case-cruncher." While he understood the futility of "attempts to concoct a unified theory of the whole"[27] of law, he did not therefore dismiss the importance of legal theory. Hardly. For Gilmore, the idea was not to dispense with theory but rather "to keep our theories open-ended, our assumptions tentative, [and] our reactions flexible."[28] Having just emphasized the obvious, I want to call attention to a more subtle and more speculative point, what I view as an undercurrent in Gilmore's thought as presented in *The Death of Contract*.

That Gilmore was critical of grand theories does not necessarily mean that he denied their value in the scheme of the everyday workings of mortals. I wonder whether he may have seen such "curious" or "monstrous" (p. 19) theories as a necessary evil, one that makes life—and life in the law—livable, or seem so. Law is a part of a larger cyclical process, running to and fro from classicism to romanticism, from order to chaos, from clarity to confusion (p. 111). Just as this process needed a doctrinaire figure like Samuel Williston to point the way back to "righteousness, discipline, order" (p. 112), so too it needed a realist figure such as Karl Llewellyn to save it from the excesses of the great system builders.[29] Builder and leveler were part of the process, each playing out his or her respective role. Thus, in time, romantic energy would spend itself; its heroes would "deny the existence of any rules" (p. 111). That would bring new problems and responses. A classical reformulation of some sort would then develop to repair the rupture.[30] The rest is history . . . waiting to be written.

More could be offered here. We have yet, however, to turn to Gilmore's text. Once done, there will be sufficient time to study the subtle, to look for undercurrents. Meanwhile, it is enough to have raised an eyebrow.

> Death plucks my ear and says, "Live—I am coming."
> —*Oliver Wendell Holmes, Jr.*
> *(March 6, 1931, radio address)*

Some have hailed Grant Gilmore as "one of the major actors in twentieth century law."[31] Still, his little tract (his *contract*, if you will) has been branded a work of "perverse dictum."[32] Some few others have been equally generous: "Professor Gilmore has been imprecise, injudicious, or just plain mistaken."[33] There it is: love-hate; praise-condemnation. It would not be fitting, at least not for these preliminary purposes, to attempt to counter this last set of criticisms beyond what has already been tendered. Suffice it to suggest that *The Death of Contract* is one of a few books in the law that does not seem to go away. It is rather like a Socratic gadfly, always there, always irritating, always making us aware of just those things we tend to disregard. It is a sting that stirs the mind. Perhaps this accounts for so much of its lasting and varied fame.

"He was a man more given to questions than to answers, more taken with seeking than finding, . . . a man of understanding and a man of wit."[34] So Gilmore once wrote of Llewellyn, the intellectual father of legal realism. That is as fair as any a sketch of Grant Gilmore and his complex life mission, including the turns it took in his famous little work. Hence this suggestion: *The Death of Contract* is more a book of beginnings than endings, more a book of wonder than conclusion; and certainly more a book for the young and bold of heart than for the old and timid of spirit.

The Death of Contract, like *The Common Law*, now belongs to a new generation. Both works, true to their nature, wait to be beckoned back to life on the lips of the living. Think of this discourse-after-death as Holmes's consideration and Gilmore's grant.

Ronald K. L. Collins
Takoma Park, Maryland
29 March 1995

In the spirit of the original work, what follows is essentially faithful to the first publication except that a bibliography and additional index references have been added, a few typographical errors have been corrected, and section headings have been added to the notes. The *Restatement of the Law (Second) Contracts* was not published until 1981, some seven years after *The Death of Contract* first appeared in print. Gilmore's references to the *Second Restatement* were thus to various *Tentative* drafts. In order to assist today's readers, I have added bracketed references, when necessary, to the Official Text (1981) version of the *Second Restatement* based on the conversion tables in volume 3 of that work. Finally, I note with appreciation the quite useful help of H.A.L., Peter Linzer, David Skover, and Jean Braucher.

Notes

1. Letter from Oliver Wendell Holmes Jr. to Joaquim Nabuco, January 3, 1908.

2. See generally Grant Gilmore, *The Ages of American Law* (Yale University Press, 1977) 68–98. The same expression can be found in Marshall McLuhan's *Understanding Media* (McGraw-Hill, 1964) 5 ("This Is the Age of Anxiety . . .").

3. Throughout, I use the word "tract" with *some* playfulness. In one respect, Gilmore's little book was not à tract insofar as it challenged the very notion of certainty so commonplace in legal tracts. In another respect, however, it was a tract of sorts insofar as its own form and argument had a tract-like quality. This more literary point is explored in my essay, *Gilmore's Grant,* listed in the bibliography.

4. In this particular respect, *The Death of Contract* was similar to *The Common Law.* Consider what is said in Professor Mark DeWolfe Howe's superb introduction to Oliver Wendell Holmes, *The Common Law* xxvi (Little, Brown, 1963).

5. Despite Gilmore's differences with Holmes's thought, he nevertheless admired the mind of the great judge. See, e.g., *The Ages of American Law, supra* note 2, at 126–127, n. 13.

6. Mark DeWolfe Howe, ed., *The Occasional Speeches of Justice Oliver Wendell Holmes* 28 (Harvard University Press, 1962).

7. See generally Grant Gilmore, *The Truth about Harvard and Yale,* Yale Law Report 8 (Winter 1963).

8. Re this biographical point and others mentioned in this foreword, see my essay *Gilmore's Grant.*

9. See Grant Gilmore, *What Is a Law School?* 15 Conn. L. Rev. 1 (1982).

10. Guido Calabresi, *Grant Gilmore and the Golden Age*, 92 Yale L.J. 1, 3 (1982). Professor Calabresi, a renowned torts professor, later served as dean of the Yale Law School and is currently a federal circuit judge.

11. Anthony T. Kronman, *What Grant Gilmore Taught*, 92 Yale L.J. 6, 7 (1982). Kronman, a former Gilmore student, served as a Yale law professor and more recently has become dean. He is one of the coauthors of the third edition of what was formerly the Kessler and Gilmore contracts casebook.

12. Friedrich Kessler, *Grant Gilmore As I Remember Him*, 92 Yale L.J. 4, 4 (1982). As of this writing, Professor Kessler has retired from Yale and lives in California.

13. See *The Truth about Harvard and Yale*, supra note 7, at p. 8.

14. Consider generally Richard Bell, ed., *Simone Weil's Philosophy of Culture* 235–59 (Cambridge University Press, 1993).

15. See, e.g., Grant Gilmore, *Stéphane Mallarmé: A Biography and Interpretation* iii, 45, 253 (1936 Ph.D. dissertation, Yale University); *The Ages of American Law*, supra note 2, at 128, n. 21. See generally *Stéphane Mallarmé*, at 242, n. 35 (re Gilmore's comments on how to read and appreciate Mallarmé); and my essay listed in the bibliography.

16. *Stéphane Mallarmé*, supra note 15, at 254.

17. Richard Epstein, Book Review, 20 Am. J. Legal Hist. 68, 72 (1976). For a wonderful account of Gilmore and Epstein, see *The Glass Menagerie: A Journal Published by Students* 46 (University of Chicago Law School, 1973).

18. *The Ages of American Law*, supra note 2, at 126 n. 8.

19. *Id.*, at 100.

20. Ellen A. Peters, *Grant Gilmore and the Illusion of Certainty,* 92 Yale L.J. 8, 8 (1982). Accord, Grant Gilmore, *Friedrich Kessler,* 84 Yale L.J. 672, 680–81 (1975). Among other things, Ellen Peters is today the chief justice of the Connecticut Supreme Court. She once taught commercial law at Yale and served as an adviser for the American Law Institute, *Restatement of the Law (Second) Contracts.*

21. Grant Gilmore, Book Review, 39 U. of Chi. L. Rev. 244, 244–45 (1971).

22. Consider Grant Gilmore, *Security Interests in Personal Property,* vol. 2, p. 1213 (1965) (re Gilmore's views on housewives).

23. *The Ages of American Law, supra* note 2, at 147, n. 11.

24. See *id.* (passing comment on and reference to Ian Macneil's *The Many Futures of Contracts,* 47 S. Calif. L. Rev. 691 (1974)).

25. See Robert A. Hillman, *The Crisis in Modern Contract Theory,* 67 Texas L. Rev. 103, 127 (1988) (an instructive and sober introduction to the subject of contemporary American contract theory by a philosophically middle-of-the-road legal scholar). The epigraph to this section is from *id.,* at 122.

26. Grant Gilmore, Book Review, 7 J. Legal Ed. 97 (1954) (reviewing John Hannold's 1954 casebook on the law of sales and sales financing).

27. Hillman, *The Crisis in Modern Contract Theory, supra* note 25, at 133.

28. *The Ages of American Law, supra* note 2, at 110.

29. See also Karl Llewellyn, *On the Complexity of Consideration,* 41 Colum. L. Rev. 777, 782 (1941). To put the point a little

differently, just as our commercial law needed a *relatively* rigid Article 9 of Secured Transactions, so also it needed a more fluid Article 2 of Sales. Gilmore, one of the key drafters of Article 9, was duly aware of this. See, e.g., *The Ages of American Law, supra* note 2, at 140–41, n. 38.

30. See generally Grant Gilmore, *Legal Realism: Its Cause and Cure*, 70 Yale L.J. 1037, 1048 (1961) ("Law cannot be, since society never is, stable. A system which works well for a generation or a century must sooner or later come in for repairs. [This is what I call] the process of renewal.").

31. Joseph M. Perillo, *Twelve Letters from Arthur L. Corbin to Robert Braucher Annotated*, 50 Wash. & Lee L. Rev. 755, 761 n. 22 (1993).

32. Robert Braucher, *Contracts*, in Bernard Schwartz, ed., *American Law: The Third Century* 121, 122 (Fred B. Rothman, 1976). Justice Braucher's statement was, "I am not at all shaken by Gilmore's perverse dictum that Contract is dead."

33. Richard Danzig, *The Death of Contract and the Life of the Profession: Observations on the Intellectual State of Legal Academia*, 29 Stan. L. Rev. 1125, 1134 (1977). The text of the full Danzig statement reads: "Too many scholars have been at too much pain to record in which ways Professor Gilmore has been imprecise, injudicious, or just plain mistaken. None of the criticism is inapt in and of itself." Danzig was a student at Yale Law School, where he studied under "two wonderful teachers," Ellen Peters and Friedrich Kessler. See Richard Danzig, *The Capability Problem in Contract Law* vii (Foundation Press, 1978).

34. Grant Gilmore, *In Memoriam: Karl Llewellyn*, 71 Yale L.J. 813, 815 (1962).

PREFACE

THIS BOOK is based on lectures which were delivered at the Ohio State University Law School, in April, 1970. In revising and expanding the lectures for publication, I have retained the somewhat informal style which initially seemed appropriate for material meant to be listened to instead of read. I found that the lecture format presented one unanticipated difficulty when it came to turning the lectures into a book. A lecturer, out of sympathy for his audience, naturally tries to make his statement as simple and uncomplicated as possible. He avoids qualifications, refinements, and collateral developments which, although they might be both relevant and interesting, would be immensely confusing to any audience. He is also under a time limitation: whatever he has to say must be said in so many hours of fifty minutes each. There is, however, no reason why the excluded material should not be restored when the lectures are printed. When I endeavored to do this, I discovered that the original text no longer opened to accommodate many of my proposed additions. Being loath to scrap what I had and start over from scratch, I found myself resorting to the doubtful expedient of putting what could not be made to fit into the text into discursive footnotes. It has always been my thought that an author should say whatever he has to say in text and use footnotes only for documentation. For the reason indicated, I have on this occasion lamentably offended against that desirable practice. The reader who is content with the bare bones of the argument will find the text self-sufficient; the footnotes have occasionally been used to put a little flesh on the bones.

I wish to thank the Dean and faculty of the Law School for having provided me with a forum and for their warm and generous hospitality during my stay in Columbus.

Grant Gilmore
Sterling Professor of Law
Yale Law School

Introduction

WE ARE TOLD that Contract, like God, is dead. And so it is. Indeed the point is hardly worth arguing anymore. The leaders of the Contract is Dead movement go on to say that Contract, being dead, is no longer a fit or worthwhile subject of study. Law students should be dispensed from the accomplishment of antiquarian exercises in and about the theory of consideration. Legal scholars should, the fact of death having been recorded, turn their attention elsewhere. They should, it is said, observe the current scene and write down a description of what they see. They should engage in sociological analysis rather than in historical or philosophical synthesis.[1] It is at this point that I find myself not so much in disagreement with their aims as completely uninterested in what they are doing.

Describing what you see is undoubtedly a useful exercise. It trains the mind in habits of close observation, precise analysis and lucid statement. It is not every lawyer who can state a complicated case accurately and well. However, when you have finished describing something, all you really

1

have is a list. In itself the list is meaningless—a lot of trees waiting for someone to assemble them into a forest. The list takes on meaning only as it is related to other lists. The materials which, as lawyers, we deal with are, as we are all too unhappily aware, forever changing—they dissolve and recombine and metamorphose into their own opposites, all, it seems, without a moment's notice. The static models, so dear to the hearts of the economists, are not for us. The present all too soon becomes the past. The future, which is surely one of the things we are concerned with, remains impenetrable. In plotting our course, the best we have to go by is some knowledge of where we have come from. The most lovingly detailed knowledge of the present state of things— the most up-to-the-minute list—begins to become useful to us only when we are in a position to compare it with what we know about what was going on last year and the year before that and so on back through the floating mists of time. At best, of course, we know the past imperfectly. No matter how many artifacts we may assemble and catalog and arrange in our museums, none of us will ever be able to think like a Roman lawyer or a medieval jurist or a nineteenth century positivist. Our late twentieth-century vision necessarily distorts what lies behind us. We are not scientists— not even social scientists—nor were meant to be. Let us not be overly depressed at that not altogether depressing thought.

If indeed it is true that Contract was alive and well in the nineteenth century and has been dying a lingering death these fifty years past, it may be that the most urgent question we can put to ourselves and to our students is: Whatever happened to the doctrine of consideration? At all events, that and related questions are what I propose to discuss with you in these lectures.

I

Origins

THIS IS by way of being a centennial year. It was just a
hundred years ago that Christopher Columbus Langdell,
like his namesake four centuries earlier, set sail over un-
charted seas and inadvertently discovered a New World.[2]
Western civilization had done very nicely for several
millenia without anyone knowing that two undiscovered
continents were interposed between Europe and Asia. It may
be that we would all be better off if the first Columbus, as the
result of a series of absurd miscalculations,[3] had not revealed
the truth. In somewhat the same way the common law had
done very nicely for several centuries without anyone realiz-
ing that there was such a thing as the law of contracts. Once
its existence had been pointed out, however, it was no more
possible for the legal mind to do without it than it would
have been for the inhabitants of Western Europe to have ex-
orcised from their collective imagination the troubling
dream of the Americas.

There is all the difference in the world between doing

something naturally or instinctively—like breathing or speaking prose—and doing the same thing with a conscious awareness of what it is that we are doing. Once it has been revealed to us that it is really prose that we are speaking, we immediately become concerned about a theory of language, about rules of grammar and syntax, about differentiating good usage from bad. Courts had, of course, been deciding cases about contracts ever since there had been courts. But the idea that there was such a thing as a general law—or theory—of contract seems never to have occurred to the legal mind until Langdell somehow stumbled across it. It remained, of course, for Langdell's successors to organize the great discovery, to map its outlines, and to plot its contours. In this country the great organizers were Holmes in his astonishing series of lectures on Contracts in *The Common Law* (1881) and Williston in his magisterial treatise.[4] In Corbin's even greater treatise[5] the process of decay and disintegration was already apparent.

It appears that, before addressing ourselves to the mystery of the death of contract, we must spend some time on what may be the even greater mystery of its birth.

In a remarkable recent book, Professor Lawrence Friedman has contributed some novel insights into the nature of what he calls the "pure" or "classical" theory of contract, by which he refers to the theory as it developed in the nineteenth century. I shall quote Professor Friedman at some length:

Basically, then, the "pure" law of contract is an area of what we can call abstract relationships. "Pure" contract doc-

6

trine is blind to details of subject matter and person. It does not ask who buys and who sells, and what is bought and sold. . . . Contract law is abstraction—what is left in the law relating to agreements when all particularities of person and subject-matter are removed.

. . . The abstraction of classical contract law is not unrealistic; it is a deliberate renunciation of the particular, a deliberate relinquishment of the temptation to restrict untrammeled individual autonomy or the completely free market in the name of social policy. The law of contract is, therefore, roughly coextensive with the free market. Liberal nineteenth century economics fits in neatly with the law of contracts so viewed. It, too, had the abstracting habit. In both theoretical models—that of the law of contracts and that of liberal economics—parties could be treated as individual economic units which in theory, enjoyed complete mobility and freedom of decision. . . .

. . . [T]he law of contract concerns and provides liberal support for the residue of economic behavior left unregulated (the free market). . . . Contract law expanded and narrowed its applicability to human affairs primarily through a process of inclusion and exclusion. The rules themselves changed less than the areas covered by them. . . . By definition, no revolution could take place because contract law acted as a residual category, its content determined mainly by what law did in other respects affecting economic behavior. Instead, types of transactions marched in and out of the area of contract. In the early part of the nineteenth century, the law of contract grew fat with the spoils of other fields. . . . The most dramatic changes touching the significance of contract law in modern life also came about, not through internal developments in contract law, but through developments in public policy which systematically robbed contract of its subject-matter . . . [such as] labor law, anti-trust law, insurance law, business regulation, and social welfare legislation. The growth of these specialized bodies of public policy removed from "contract" (in the sense of abstract relationships) transactions and situations formerly governed by it. . . .[6]

Thus Professor Friedman. Although we shall depart from his analysis at some points, we may retain as central ideas the concept of the general law of contract as a residual category—what is left over after all the "specialized" bodies of law have been added up—highly abstract, in close historical relationship with the free market of classical economic theory,[7] a theoretical construct which, having little or nothing to do with the real world, would not—or could not—change as the real world changed.[8] Professor Friedman goes on to comment on another significant aspect of the contract construct—which is that it resisted, and continues to resist, codification long after most, if not all, of the fields of law apparently most closely related to it had passed under the statutory yoke.[9] We must indeed provide ourselves at some point with an explanation of why it was that, instead of a Uniform Contracts Act, we got a *Restatement of Contracts.*

Asked to locate the law of contract on the legal spectrum, most of us, I assume, would place it in the area usually denominated Commercial Law. It is true that our unitary contract theory has always had an uncomfortable way of spilling over into distinctly non-commercial situations and that what may be good for General Motors does not always make sense when applied to charitable subscriptions, antenuptial agreements and promises to convey the family farm provided the children will support the old people for life. But we feel instinctively that commercial law is the heart of the matter and that, the need arising, the commercial rules can be applied over, with whatever degree of disingenuity may be required, to fit, for example, the case of King Lear and his unruly daughters.

We use the term "commercial law" in a curiously restrictive sense. Commercial law, to lawyers, means the law relating to the sale and distribution of goods—thus, the law of sales, the law of carriers, the law of shipping; to the modes of extending credit and making payment for goods sold—thus, the law of negotiable instruments; and to the methods of financing credit transactions on the security of the goods sold—thus, the whole involved network of personal property security law. In a word, this is the law which the Industrial Revolution left in its wake. Until the late eighteenth century there was no such thing as a law of sales or a law of negotiable instruments—not to mention a law of contracts. Before then there were cases about sales and cases about negotiable instruments—as there were cases about contracts. But cases are one thing and a systematically organized, sharply differentiated body of law is quite another thing.[10]

There are few things more fascinating in our jurisprudence than the organization of what comes, almost immediately, to be perceived as a new "field" of law. This phenomenon takes place in response to dramatic shifts in the technological, political and cultural organization of our society. Law, by its nature, reflects what is—not, except to the extent dictated by the idea of cultural lag, what was and never will be. If seashells are currency, we will have a detailed, intricate and comprehensive law of wampum; if seashells cease to be currency, the law of wampum will gradually die and be forgotten. Until goods, and claims to money based on their manufacture and sale, became as significant a repository of wealth as real property had traditionally been, we had no need for a law of sales or a law of negotiable instruments. The need arising, the law was promptly provided.

Indeed it was provided with startling rapidity. In not much more than half a century the main outlines of what we call commercial law had been laid down and many of the subsidiary details worked out. That something extraordinary had occurred was apparent to observers of the time. Thus in 1837 Justice Joseph Story delivered to the Governor of Massachusetts a Report on the Codification of the Common Law, written on behalf of a commission appointed to consider "the practicability and expediency of reducing to a written and systematic code the common law of Massachusetts."[11] A comprehensive Code—all the law about everything—would be, Story wrote for the Commissioners, "either positively mischievous, or inefficacious, or futile."[12] On the other hand there were certain areas in the substantive law whose codification was both possible and desirable. The law of what Story called "commercial contracts" was "eminently . . . in this predicament":

. . . [U]nder the forming hands of a succession of learned judges and jurists for the last century, they have attained a scientific precision, and accuracy, and clearness, which give them an indisputable title to be treated as a fixed system of national jurisprudence. In regard to commercial contracts, it may be affirmed without hesitation, that the general principles which define and regulate them, and even the subordinate details of those principles, to a very great extent, are now capable of being put in a regular order, and announced in determinate propositions in the text of a code. Among these contracts, the Commissioners would especially recommend as the subjects of a code the following titles, viz.: the law of agency, of bailments, of guaranty, of suretyship, of bills of exchange, or promissory notes, of insurance, and of partnership. They would also recommend, in like manner, the law of navigation and shipping and maritime contracts, including therein the law respecting the rights, duties and authorities of owners and part-owners, and masters, and seamen, and shippers, and passengers; the law of bottomry, of charterparties, bills of lading, and other contracts of affreightment, including therein the law of freight; and the law of general average, of salvage, and of seamen's wages. . . .[13]

I call your particular attention to the list of subjects which Story felt could be "announced in determinate propositions in the text of a code." He includes within the area of "commercial contracts," as we would not, the law of business organizations—agency and partnership although not, interestingly enough, the as yet embryonic corporation.

Promissory notes and bills of exchange make their expected appearance. Financing and security transactions show up in the references to bailments (which included pledge), guaranty and suretyship. Finally there is insurance—by which he evidently meant marine insurance—and maritime or shipping law which gets the most detailed treatment of all. There is no reference to a law of "sales," as such. That, curiously, came along a generation later. The first American treatise on Sales came out in 1848, having been written by Justice Story's son, William Wetmore Story, who, after that act of filial piety, abandoned the law and spent the rest of a long life as a sculptor in Italy. The treatise on Sales is, by the way, very fine indeed and so, for all I know, the sculptures are too.[14]

For Story, then, there was no such thing as a generalized law of—or theory of—contract. There were specialized bodies of law which had sprung up to regulate the various aspects of commercial transactions which had, with the Industrial Revolution, assumed paramount importance in our social and economic life. Story, indeed, during his astonishingly productive career, wrote treatises on most of these specialized bodies of law;[15] it never occurred to him to write a treatise on "Contracts."[16]

Without giving much thought to the matter, we have tended to assume that "Contract" came first, and then, in time, the various specialties—negotiable instruments, sales, insurance and so on—split off from the main trunk.[17] The truth seems to be the other way around. The specialties were fully developed—indeed, in the case of negotiable instruments law, already frozen in a premature old age[18]—

long before the need for a general theory of contract had occurred to anyone. Once the theory had been announced it did operate, by a sort of backlash effect, to influence further developments in some of the specialties—particularly sales.[19]

I have credited Dean Langdell with the almost inadvertent discovery of the general theory of Contract. The reference was to his pioneering casebook on Contracts which appeared just a hundred years ago and, even more, to the "Summary of the Law of Contracts" which he added as an appendix to the second edition of the casebook in 1880. It has been said that an infallible prescription for becoming a great man is to live a long time. Langdell lived a long time. We know little about him and almost nothing about his curious choice of Contracts as the subject-matter of the very first casebook of all.[20] He believed that the law was a science, like any other science—an attitude which commended him to President Eliot of Harvard, himself a chemist, and led to Langdell's appointment as the first Dean of the Harvard Law School.[21] In the preface to the casebook Langdell wrote:

> Law, considered as a science, consists of certain principles and doctrines. . . . [T]he number of fundamental legal doctrines is much less than is commonly supposed; the many different guises in which the same doctrine is constantly making its appearance, and the great extent to which legal treatises are a repetition of each other, being the cause of much misapprehension. . . . It seemed to me, therefore, to be possible to take such a branch of the law as Contracts, for example, and, without exceeding comparatively moderate

13

limits, to select, classify and arrange all the cases which had contributed in any important degree to the growth, development, or establishment of any of its essential doctrines. . . .[22]

To judge by the casebook and the Summary, Langdell was an industrious researcher of no distinction whatever either of mind or, as the passage I have just quoted may have suggested, of style. But it is with Langdell that, for the first time, we see Contract as, in Professor Friedman's term,[23] an "abstraction"—a remote, impersonal, bloodless abstraction. The three principal chapters into which the casebook is divided are entitled: Mutual Assent, Consideration and Conditional Contracts: we are evidently at a far remove from Story's list of "commercial contracts."[24] The casebook, according to Langdell, was to contain—and presumably did contain—all the important contract cases that had ever been decided. "All the cases" turned out to be mostly English cases, arranged in historical sequence from the seventeenth century down to the date of publication; the English cases were occasionally supplemented by comparable sequences of cases from New York and Massachusetts—no other American jurisdictions being represented. The Summary, which runs to a hundred and fifty pages or so, is devoted almost entirely to explaining which of the cases in the main part of the casebook are "right" and which are "wrong." The explanation, typically, is dogmatic rather than reasoned; Langdell knew right from wrong, no doubt by divine revelation, and that should suffice for the student. This aspect of the Summary of the Law of Contracts throws an entertaining light on the origins of case-method teaching. At least in Langdell's version, it had nothing whatever to do with getting students to think for themselves; it was, on the contrary, a method of indoctrination through brainwashing.

Langdell, then, did little more than launch the idea that there was—or should be—such a thing as a general theory of contract. The theory itself was pieced together by his successors—notably Holmes, in broad philosophical outline, and Williston, in meticulous, although not always accurate, scholarly detail. At this point it is necessary to give some idea of the content of what we may call the Holmes-Williston construct—which I shall attempt to do impressionistically rather than scientifically. Having accomplished that chore, we can return to the far more interesting business of speculating on why Langdell's idea, brilliantly reformulated by Holmes, had the fabulous success it did instead of going down the drain into oblivion as a hundred better ideas than Langdell's do every day of the week.

The theory seems to have been dedicated to the proposition that, ideally, no one should be liable to anyone for anything.[25] Since the ideal was not attainable, the compromise solution was to restrict liability within the narrowest possible limits. Within those limits, however, liability was to be absolute: as Holmes put it, "The only universal consequence of a legally binding promise is, that the law makes the promisor pay damages if the promised event does not come to pass."[26] Liability, although absolute—at least in theory—was nevertheless, to be severely limited. The equitable remedy of specific performance was to be avoided so far as possible—no doubt we would all be better off if Lord Coke's views had prevailed in the seventeenth century and the equitable remedy had never developed at all.[27] Money damages for breach of contract were to be "compensatory," never punitive; the contract-breaker's motivation, Holmes explained, makes no legal difference whatever and indeed every man has a right "to break his contract if he chooses"[28] — that is, a right to elect to pay damages instead of performing his contractual obligation. Therefore the wicked contract-breaker should pay no more in damages than the innocent and the pure in heart. The "compensatory" damages, which were theoretically recoverable, turned out to be a good deal less than enough to compensate the victim for the losses which in fact he might have suffered. Damages in contract, it was pointed out, were one thing and damages in tort another; the contract-breaker was not to be held responsible, as the tortfeasor was, for all the consequences of his actions. Another aspect of the theory was that the courts should operate as detached umpires or referees, doing no more than to see that the rules of the game were observed and refusing to intervene affirmatively to see that justice or anything of that sort was done. Courts do not, it was said, make contracts for the parties. The parties themselves must see that the last i is properly dotted, the last t properly crossed; the courts will not do it for them. And if A, without the protection of a binding contract, improvidently relies, to his detriment, on B's promises and assurances, that may be unfortunate for A but is no fit matter for legal concern. Contract liability, furthermore, was to be sharply differentiated from tort liability and there was to be no softening or blurring of the harsh limitations of contract theory by the recognition of an intermediate no-man's-land between contract and tort; the idea which later flourished as "quasi-contract" was no part of the Holmesian theory.

It is, I think, necessary to make the point that, according to Holmes, tort liability, like contract liability, should be narrowly restricted. The development of a general theory of torts came almost simultaneously with that of the general theory of contract, although the reasons for the late development of a tort theory seem to have been of a somewhat different order from those that accounted for the phenomenon on the contract side. In tort the proliferation of the common law forms of action seems to have inhibited generalization: there was a theory of trespass, a theory of case, a theory of deceit and so on. Holmes, whose contribution to the formulation of contract theory we shall presently examine in detail, was also one of the first to attempt to formulate a generalized theory of tort.

The proposition that, ideally, no one should be liable to anyone for anything comes through even more dramatically in Holmes's lectures on torts in *The Common Law* than in the subsequent lectures on Contracts. He begins the argument by briefly dismissing Austin's theory of law as a sanction, with liability based on "personal fault." He then comments that another theory, directly opposed to Austin's and "adopted by some of the greatest common-law authorities" (none of whom is named), "requires serious discussion before it can be set aside in favor of any third opinion which may be maintained." This view, which is obviously to be "set aside" after a "serious discussion," is that: "under the common law a man *acts* at his peril."[29] We then get nine pages of closely reasoned discussion designed to demonstrate that there never was such a rule at common law. At that point, with breathtaking abruptness, Holmes, without citation of authority, unveils his own "third opinion":

> The general principle of our law is that loss from accident must lie where it falls. . . .

In developing this astonishing principle of no liability for harm done to other people or their property, he comments:

> A man need not, it is true, do this or that act—the term *act* implies a choice,—but he must act somehow. Furthermore, the public generally profits by individual activity. As action cannot be avoided, and tends to the public good, there is obviously no policy in throwing the hazard of what is at once desirable and inevitable upon the actor.[30]

Holmes, a realist, recognized that the principle that "loss . . . must lie where it falls" so that socially useful "action" would not be discouraged could not be perfectly realized. He had started by rejecting the Austinian idea that liability was, or should be, based on "personal fault" or "a state of the party's mind." His proposed alternative was that liability should be based on an "objective" failure of the alleged tortfeasor's behavior to measure up to the accepted standards of the community. Although the law of torts, as he noted, "abounds in moral phraseology," the progress of jurisprudence lay in freeing tort law from the unnecessary and misleading overlay of moral sententiousness. Throughout the

18

torts lectures Holmes's evident concern is to convince his listeners (and later his readers) that common law concepts of liability should be cut back, wherever possible, and in no event allowed to expand.[31]

From this necessary digression we may return to our study of the theory of contract.

Where did the idea for this curious—one is tempted to say, monstrous—machine come from? It is fair to say that the theory of contract did not come as the natural result of a continuing case-law development; in fact it represented a sharp break with the past, even the recent past. The inventors of the theory did not make it all up out of their own heads. Indeed they made industrious use of whatever bits and pieces of case law, old and new, could be made to fit the theory. Such cases were immediately promoted to "leading cases" and made to fit—in much the same way that Procrustes made his guests fit. Cases which could not be made to fit were ignored or dismissed, with Langdellian certitude, as "wrong." On the whole, however, the theory was in its origins, and continued to be during its life, an ivory tower abstraction. Its natural habitat was the law schools, not the law courts. And yet, in following this line, we must not lose sight of the fact—the crucial fact—that the theory was an instant and spectacular success. In its "pure" form the theory may never have existed outside the classrooms of the Harvard Law School. But generations of lawyers and judges and law professors grew up believing that the theory was true—and it is our beliefs, however absurd, that condition our actions.

The balance-wheel of the great machine was the theory

of consideration, newly reformulated and put to some hitherto unsuspected uses. The word "consideration" has been around for a long time, so it is tempting to think that we have had a theory of consideration for a long time. In fact until the nineteenth century the word never acquired any particular meaning or stood for any theory. In the late eighteenth century, indeed, Lord Mansfield suggested that in English law, as in the civil law, all promises seriously made should be taken as legally binding,[32] subject to a broad theory of what might be called invalidating cause or excuse for fraud, duress, coercion, and, perhaps, change of circumstance. It is true that these suggestions were rejected within a half century of Mansfield's death.[33] With the rejection it became customary to look on Mansfield's heresies as a curious aberration, explainable perhaps on the ground of his Scottish birth, on the part of an otherwise great judge. It may be that there was less aberration and more sense—even more sense of history—on Mansfield's side than on the side of his later critics. Meanwhile, the English courts, having rejected Mansfield, began trying to explain—really for the first time—what they thought consideration meant. A formula which became fashionable put it in terms of benefit and detriment. If a promisor received any benefit from a transaction, that was sufficient consideration to support his promise. On the other hand, if a promisee suffered any detriment, that, likewise, was sufficient to support the promise. Any benefit would do; any detriment would do.[34] Indeed, in most of the early formulations of the benefit-detriment theory of consideration, the only class of promises which would have been denied enforceability would have been gift promises, not relied on by the promises.

The new day dawned with Holmes. I shall quote several passages from his lecture on The Elements of Contract:

> It is said that any benefit conferred by the promisee on the promisor, or any detriment incurred by the promisee, may be a consideration. It is also thought that every consideration may be reduced to a case of the latter sort, using the word "detriment" in a somewhat broad sense. . . .
>
> It appears to me that it has not always been sufficiently borne in mind that the same thing may be a consideration or not, as it is dealt with by the parties. . . .
>
> . . . It is hard to see the propriety of erecting any detriment which an instrument may disclose or provide for, into a consideration, unless the parties have dealt with it on that footing. In many cases a promisee may incur a detriment without thereby furnishing a consideration. The detriment may be nothing but a condition precedent to performance, as where a man promises another to pay him five hundred dollars if he breaks his leg.
>
> It is said that consideration must not be confounded with motive. It is true that it must not be confounded with what may be the prevailing or chief motive in actual fact. A man may promise to paint a picture for five hundred dollars, while his chief motive may be a desire for fame. A consideration may be given and accepted, in fact, solely for the purpose of making a promise binding. But, nevertheless, it is the essence of a consideration, that, by the terms of the agreement, it is

given and accepted as the motive or inducement for furnishing the consideration. The root of the whole matter is the relation of reciprocal conventional inducement, each for the other, between consideration and promise.[35]

Now the vulgar error that any benefit or any detriment would do has been exploded. It is clear that there are benefits and benefits, detriments and detriments. No matter how much detriment a promisee may have suffered, he has not, thereby, necessarily furnished a consideration. Nor does he have, so far as Holmes takes us, any right to redress or even any claim on our sympathies, no matter how reasonable his detrimental reliance may have been, not even if, in the course of incurring his detriment, he has conferred a benefit on the other party. Absent "consideration," the unhappy promisee has no right or claim. And nothing is "consideration" unless "the parties have dealt with it on that footing." There must be, in the final mysterious phrase, "the relation of reciprocal conventional inducement, each for the other, between consideration and promise." That indeed is "the root of the whole matter."

It seems perfectly clear that Holmes was, quite consciously, proposing revolutionary doctrine[36] and was not in the least interested in stating or restating the common law as it was. He was, at the time he wrote the lectures which make up *The Common Law*, as learned in the history of the law—including the law of contracts—as any lawyer in the English-speaking world.[37] Yet his analysis of the true meaning of "consideration" comes forth almost naked of citation of authority or precedent.[38] He starts with an off-hand reference to what is commonly "said" and commonly "thought." However, what is clear to Holmes "has not always been sufficiently borne in mind" by others. Whereupon, we are off to the races at a dizzying clip.

There is never any point in arguing with a successful revolution. What Holmes told the young lawyers who flocked to his lectures in the spring of 1881 promptly became the truth—the indisputable truth—of the matter for his own and succeeding generations.[39] The "bargain" theory of consideration, proposed by Holmes, is enshrined in the definition of consideration in § 75 of the original *Restatement of Contracts*—about which we shall have more to say later—and is indeed carried forward in the current tentative drafts of the second *Restatement* [§ 71 in the 1981 Official Text].[40]

With the Holmesian formulation, consideration became a tool for narrowing the range of contractual liability. "The whole doctrine of contract," he noted in this connection, "is formal and external."[41] Unless the formalities were accomplished, there could be no contract and, consequently, no liability.[42] The austerity of doctrine would not be tempered for the shorn lambs who might shiver in its blast.

The theoretical basis having thus been provided, the next step was the extension of the newly minted theory of consideration to the entire life-history of a contract, from birth to death. Consideration theory was used to explain why offers, even if they are expressed to be irrevocable, are in their nature necessarily revocable at any time before acceptance —why modifications of going contracts under which A promises to pay B more than the originally agreed contract price for doing the work are not binding on A—why agreements by creditors to discharge their debtors on payment of less than the amount due are not binding on the creditors.[43] For the result in each of these situations there was indeed some case law precedent, past or current, but accommodation of the cases to the newfangled theory required something like major surgery on the cases themselves. By the end of the century the "rule" of *Dickinson v. Dodds*[44]—which was chosen as "leading" case on the revocability of offers— the "rule" of *Stilk v. Myrick*[45] on modifications, the "rule" of *Foakes v. Beer*[46] on discharges had been generalized into abstractions that had little or nothing to do with the cases themselves.

In *Stilk v. Myrick* it appeared that two seamen had deserted a ship which was engaged on a Russian voyage. The master was unable to replace the deserters at Cronstadt where the ship had made port. Under these circumstances the master offered to divide the wages of the two deserters among the remaining members of the crew if they had to work the ship back to London shorthanded (as in fact they did). The owners having refused to pay the additional wages, plaintiff (one of the members of the crew) brought suit on the Cronstadt agreement. It was held by Lord Ellenborough that the action did not lie; the plaintiff and his fellows were entitled only to the wages they had originally signed on for.

Now, what is the principle or "rule" which the case is supposed to illustrate?

According to Williston:

> Where A and B have entered into a bilateral agreement, it not infrequently happens that one of the parties, becoming

dissatisfied with the contract, refuses to perform or to continue performance unless a larger compensation than that
provided in the original agreement is promised him. . . . On
principle the second agreement [i.e. the Cronstadt agreement on the *Stilk v. Myrick facts*] is invalid for the performance by the recalcitrant contractor is no legal detriment to
him whether actually given or promised, since, at the time
the second agreement was entered into, he was already
bound to do the work; nor is the performance under the second agreement a legal benefit to the promisor since he was
already entitled to have the work done. In such situations
and others identical in principle, the great weight of authority supports this conclusion.[47]

There are of course many cases, old and new, of the type
Professor Williston was hypothesizing. Was *Stilk v. Myrick*
one of them? It seems unlikely that a neutral observer, not
yet corrupted by the study of law, would jump to that conclusion. Professor Williston's case is one in which "one of the
parties, becoming dissatisfied with the contract, refuses to
perform or to continue performance" unless he is paid more
than he had originally agreed to do the work for. We are not
told that any of the complaining seamen refused to go forward with the voyage unless they received the wages of the
two deserters. It is of course possible that in real life they did
refuse to go forward unless the deserters were replaced (or
their wages distributed). Counsel, however, did not even attempt to argue that the master had been coerced or threatened. All we can gather from the reports of the case is that
the master, having found it impossible to recruit two new

hands, voluntarily offered to distribute the wages among the remaining members of the crew.

Williston's hypothetical also assumes that the "dissatisfied" party insists on the greater pay for doing the same work he had originally agreed to do for less. It is clear enough that the seamen in *Stilk v. Myrick* were doing more work on the return voyage than they had agreed to do—their own work plus the work of the two deserters. There is a doctrine of maritime law under which the members of the crew are required to exert extraordinary efforts, indeed to venture their lives, to rescue the ship from an emergency. Lord Ellenborough seems to have assumed that, under this doctrine, the seamen were required to work the ship shorthanded for their original wages. To know whether his assumption was correct, we would have to know a great deal more than we are told about the circumstances of the "desertions," about the state of the labor market in Cronstadt and about the dangers of a return voyage with less than a full crew. We do know that the ship was safe in port at Cronstadt; it was not in imminent peril from the sea. If the ambiguities in the factual situation were resolved in favor of the crew, it is quite possible that, under maritime law, they would have been justified in quitting the service of the ship at Cronstadt rather than work it back to London shorthanded. Counsel for the plaintiff made no attempt to investigate these questions. Lord Ellenborough may have been right or counsel, representing impecunious seamen with fairly small claims, may not have been as aggressive and ingenious in behalf of their clients as they should have been.

Stilk v. Myrick can hardly be described as a case in which a dissatisfied party insists on more pay for doing the same work. The next point is that Williston supports his statement of the principle quoted above with a long string citation of cases ("the great weight of authority") which begins: "Harris v. Watson, Peake, 72;[48] Stilk v. Myrick, 2 Camp. 371. . . ."[49] Williston goes on to cite dozens of cases, English and American, in support of his statement (a few cases, illustrating a "contrary view" which has prevailed "in a few jurisdictions" are collected in a separate footnote). However, from the form and style of the citation it is clear that the two English cases are given as the "root authority"—the "leading cases."

Harris v. Watson, which had been decided almost twenty years before *Stilk v. Myrick,* was another case in which seamen were attempting to collect extra wages which had been promised them by the master. Unlike *Stilk v. Myrick*, however, *Harris v. Watson* was a classical illustration of the maritime law doctrine which has been referred to. It was proved, according to the statement of the case, that, "the ship being in danger," the master "to induce the seamen to exert themselves," promised each of them an extra five guineas over and above their regular wages. Lord Kenyon briefly remarked:

If this action was to be supported, it would materially affect the navigation of this kingdom. . . . [The] rule [of maritime law] was founded on a principle of policy, for if sailors were in all events to have their wages,[50] and in times of danger were entitled to insist on an extra charge on such a promise

27

as this, they would in many cases suffer a ship to sink, unless the captain would pay any extravagant demand they might think proper to make.[51]

Harris v. Watson, it appears, was decided entirely on the rule and "policy" of the maritime law, with the realistic comment thrown in that the contrary decision would "materially affect the navigation of this kingdom."

Harris v. Watson was, naturally, the principal authority relied on by counsel for the owners in *Stilk v. Myrick*. Counsel for the plaintiff suggested the obvious distinction that the Cronstadt agreement had been made while the ship was in port and "was not made from the apprehension of danger, nor extorted from the captain; but a voluntary offer on his part for extraordinary service."[52] Lord Ellenborough, however, was not persuaded and chose to follow *Harris v. Watson*.

At this point our understanding of *Stilk v. Myrick* becomes entangled in the vagaries of early nineteenth century English case-reporting. According to the report in Espinasse,[53] Lord Ellenborough said that "he recognized the principle of the case of *Harris v. Watson* as founded on just and proper policy," noted that the *Stilk v. Myrick* seamen had signed on for the round trip voyage to the Baltic and back, not merely for the voyage to Cronstadt, and concluded that he could see no difference in principle between the two cases. If that was a correct report, there was no more thought given in *Stilk v. Myrick* to contract and consideration theory than there had been in *Harris v. Watson*; it was a pure "policy" decision based on the maritime law. However, Lord Ellenborough is quoted quite differently in the Campbell report.[54] There he is made to say:

> I think Harris v. Watson was rightly decided; but I doubt whether the ground of public policy, upon which Lord Kenyon is stated to have proceeded, be the true principle on which the decision is to be supported. Here, I say, the agreement is void for want of consideration.

After noting that the "mariners" in *Stilk v. Myrick* had signed on for the round trip voyage and giving as his opinion that they would not, under the circumstances of the case, have been "at liberty to quit the vessel at Cronstadt," he concluded:

> Therefore, without looking to the policy of this agreement, I think it is void for want of consideration. . . .

What are we to make of the discrepancy in the two reports? I have been told by English colleagues that Espinasse is not held in high regard as a reporter.[55] And it does seem unlikely that Campbell would have made up out of whole cloth the remarks about consideration which he attributes to Lord Ellenborough. If we assume that Campbell was being reasonably accurate, what explanation can there be for Lord Ellenborough's switch from the "public policy" ground on which *Harris v. Watson* had been decided to "want of consideration"? It is of course true that *Stilk v. Myrick* was decided at a time when the reaction against Lord Mansfield's attempt to uproot consideration theory[56] had already set in. "Want of consideration" as a ground for invalidating a purported contract is a phrase that would have come more readily to the mind of an English judge in 1809 (*Stilk v. Myrick*) than in 1791 (*Harris v. Watson*). It is also within the bounds of fair comment to suggest that the maritime law rule, which clearly applied to *Harris v. Watson* was, at best, of doubtful applicability on the *Stilk v. Myrick* facts. As a good common lawyer, Lord Ellenborough may have felt more comfortable with the broader ground for decision, which of course made it unnecessary for him to deal seriously with the distinction argued by counsel.[57]

After this lengthy digression we are in a position to return to the manner in which the case of *Stilk v. Myrick* was transmuted into the "rule of *Stilk v. Myrick*."[58] It was done, of course, by lumping two unlike cases together without stating the facts of either case. Of the two reports of *Stilk v. Myrick* Williston cited only the Campbell report. No mention was made of the facts that there is no conceivable way in which *Harris v. Watson* can be taken to have been decided on consideration theory (the "rule") or that there is considerable doubt as to the theory on which *Stilk v. Myrick* was decided.[59] Such is the progress of jurisprudence.

I have gone into tedious detail about *Stilk v. Myrick* because I think that the devious process by which the "cases" became the "rules" of the general theory of contract can be understood only microscopically. We need not concern ourselves with whether the process involved deliberate deception or merely unconscious distortion on the part of the theory-builders. What is clear is that some funny things happened on the way from case report to treatise.

We may dispose of our next two cases somewhat more briefly.

Dickinson v. Dodds—the revocable offer case—was current material, having been decided in 1876 in the Chancery Division of the Court of Appeal.[60] The case involved an offer to sell real property. The offer, which was made on a Wednesday, was, by the terms of a handwritten postscript, to be "left over" until Friday. Before Friday Dodds, the offeror, sold the land to Allen. Dickinson, the offeree, learned of the sale to Allen before he had accepted the Wednesday offer. Before the expiration time on Friday, but after having learned of the sale to Allen, Dickinson notified Dodds of his acceptance. *Held*: Dodds was free to revoke the offer at any time before acceptance and, consequently, was not liable to Dickinson. Now what does the case mean? In the first instance it should be noted that it is far from clear what Dickinson or Dodds or both of them meant or understood by "left over." Quite plausibly the term meant merely that Dickinson had to accept by Friday at the latest, Dodds being, meanwhile, free to withdraw if he changed his mind or got a better offer. Let us assume, however, that "left over" is properly translated as meaning: This offer is irrevocable until Friday. If, on that debatable assumption, Dodds is still held free to revoke, how is the result to be explained? Not, according to the opinions delivered in the case, on consideration theory.[61] For there to be a contract, Mellish, L.J., explained, there must be, at some moment in time, a meeting of the minds—the wills of the parties must, subjectively, concur.[62] Since Dodds had changed his mind before Dickinson got around to accepting, there was, obviously, no meeting of the minds and, obviously, no contract.[63] The result in *Dickinson v. Dodds* commended itself to the Holmesian theorists more than the facts or Mellish's reasoning did. For one thing the Holmesians, describing themselves as objectivists, had nothing but scorn for "subjective" or "meeting of the minds" theory.[64] The case was therefore restated as one involving, on the facts, an offer clearly meant to be irrevocable and the result was explained on the ground that Dodds had received no "consideration" for the assurance of irrevocability.[65]

It should be noted that the "restatement" of *Dickinson v. Dodds* in terms of consideration theory makes irrelevant what the parties may have intended by the provision that the offer should be "left over" until Friday. If, apart from the possibility of an offer under seal, all offers are revocable unless supported by what came to be called an "independent" consideration,[66] then it makes no difference, absent the consideration, in what form of language the offer may be expressed. "You may have until Friday to accept but I may revoke the offer at any time before acceptance" comes out exactly the same way as "You may have until Friday to accept and I also promise that I will not revoke the offer before Friday." Under the new dispensation the offeror is not bound by what he has said or has intended to say or has been understood to say; he is bound if, and only if, he has received a "consideration" ("consideration" being, as Holmes liked to point out, "as much a form as a seal").[67] Williston's treatment of the point is instructive.[68] He cites *Dickinson v. Dodds* as the leading case for the proposition that "offers unless under seal or given for consideration may be revoked at any time prior to the creation of a contract by acceptance." The same rule applies, he adds, "even though a definite time in which acceptance may be made, is named in such an offer. . . ." And finally "even though the offer expressly states that it shall not be withdrawn, nevertheless, it may be." Williston evidently treats the second and third propositions which I have just quoted as logical deductions from the general principle. Williston, when he wanted to, could read cases accurately; in this instance he did not bother to pretend that the subordinate propositions were directly involved in *Dickinson v. Dodds*. It was enough that they "logically" followed from it.

The last of the trio of cases—*Foakes v. Beer*[69]—was decided in the House of Lords in 1884. It is worth noting how much of the case material that was built into the theoretical structure was, at the time, current. The idea that issues of such importance as whether offers are in their nature revocable and whether creditors can effectively discharge their debtors on part payment had never been authoritatively decided in England—or for that matter in this country—until the 1870s (*Dickinson v. Dodds*) or until the 1880s (*Foakes v. Beer*) is so surprising as to make the mind boggle. I suggested earlier that Holmesian contract theory itself represented a sharp break with the past. I suggest further that the current cases, which the theorists so eagerly seized on, themselves represented breaks with past tradition. At least with respect to the American commentary on *Foakes v. Beer*, a good deal of scholarly ink has been used up in the demonstration that the learned Law Lords simply misread their cases or did not

33

know what they were talking about.[70] The point is, I think, that the judges, or some of them, were, obscurely, working along the same lines as the theorists. However much overstatement, unconscious or deliberate, may have gone into the elaboration of the "rules" that were derived from the cases, the cases did exist.[71] Once again, we must remind ourselves that anyone can state a new theory or proclaim a new truth; it is by no means the case that every new theory or every new truth sweeps all before it as, for a time, this theory and this truth did.

On its facts, *Foakes v. Beer*, like *Dickinson v. Dodds* before it, was, to say the least, ambiguous. It was by no means clear that Mrs. Beer, the judgment creditor, had ever promised to release Dr. Foakes, her debtor, from paying interest, provided that he paid the principal amount of the debt in installments over several years (as in fact he did). There are suggestions in the case that if Mrs. Beer on receipt of the last installment had given Dr. Foakes an "acquittance"—that is, an acknowledgment of payment in full—that would have been binding on her.[72] However, what came to be the most celebrated passage in the *Foakes v. Beer* opinions was Lord Blackburn's resurrection of a dictum attributed to Lord Coke in *Pinnel's Case* (1602):

> And it was resolved by the whole Court, that payment of a lesser sum on the day in satisfaction of a greater, cannot be any satisfaction for the whole, because it appears to the Judges that by no possibility, a lesser sum can be a satisfaction to the plaintiff for a greater sum: but the gift of a horse, hawk, or robe, &c, in satisfaction is good.[73]

He was persuaded, Blackburn wrote in effect, that the decision he and his colleagues were about to give was wrong but, of course, if Lord Coke had said in 1602 that a part could never be satisfaction for the whole, why that was the end of the matter. Giving effect to the dictum in *Pinnel's Case* meant disregarding what Coke had said in a later case[74] as well as a good many other holdings scattered over the ensuing two and a half centuries[75]—but, what must be, must be.

The House of Lords, evidently, had its doubts. The theorists had none, and *Foakes v. Beer*—or, rather, the rule in *Foakes v. Beer*—was promptly installed as one of the brightest jewels in the crown of the common law.[76] We may, as always, pursue the rule to its ultimate abstraction in Williston:

> Since a debtor incurs no legal detriment by paying part or all of what he owes, and a creditor obtains no legal benefit in receiving it, such a payment if made at the place where the debt is due in the medium of payment which was due, and at or after maturity of the debt, is not valid consideration for any promise. The question most commonly arises when a debtor pays part of a liquidated debt in return for the creditor's agreement that the debt shall be fully satisfied. Such an agreement on the part of the creditor needs for its support other consideration besides the mere part payment.

The rule, Williston noted, "has not infrequently been criticized by courts and law writers; and in a few jurisdictions . . . has been changed by decision or statute."[77] He concluded on a note of somewhat muted triumph:

But the rule of the common law has at least the merit of
consistency with the general rule of consideration governing
the formation and discharge of contracts.[78]

Apparently the best that could be said for the rule is that it
had "at least" the merit of being logically consistent with
other rules. So far had we departed, in the second generation
of the new dispensation, from Holmes's great epigram: "The
life of the law has not been logic: it has been experience."[79]

The reformulation of consideration theory in terms of bargain—the "reciprocal conventional inducement"[80]—seems to
have reflected itself in a series of subsidiary propositions or
slogans, all of which, to the extent that they were taken seriously, offered ways of escape from the imposition of contractual liability. One was that there can be no such thing as "an
agreement to agree"—no duty, that is, to bargain in good
faith; the contractual trap will not be sprung until the last
possible moment. Another was that there must be "mutuality of obligation"—both parties must be bound or neither
will be bound." The "mutuality of obligation" slogan modu-
lated into discussion of the nature of promises: if either of
the meshing promises could be found to be "illusory," then
neither of the meshing promises bound.[81]

The "illusory promise" variant of the "mutuality of obligation" theory led to one of the least creditable episodes in
our legal history. To go by the case reports, requirements contracts were just beginning to come into widespread use toward the end of the nineteenth century. A promises to buy
from B all his requirements of whatever-it-is for one year or

five or ten. But is not A's promise "illusory," since nobody knows what his requirements will be, or indeed, whether he will have any? To some judges—it would be pleasant to think that these were the successfully brainwashed products of Dean Langdell's course in Contracts—the objection was fatal.[82] Eventually the issue was disposed of and the sensible arrangement of a requirements deal was granted political asylum within the domain of contract—but at the cost of a generation or more of totally unnecessary litigation.[83] In such unexpected ways did the general theory of contract wreak havoc within the commercial community for whose protection it was, presumably, drawn up in the first place. The trouble was that businessmen, adapting to changing circumstance, kept doing things differently. The "general theory" required that, always and everywhere, things remain as they had, in theory, always been.

II

Development

IN THE COURSE of the preceding lecture the point was made that Holmes and his successors substituted an "objectivist" approach to the theory of contract for the "subjectivist" approach which the courts had—almost instinctively, it would seem, and without giving any thought to the matter—been following.[84] At this point we must inquire what the switch from "subjective" to "objective" involved, what difference (if any) it made in the results which the courts were supposed to arrive at and what relationship the newly minted theory of "objectivism" had to the main lines of the general theory of contract.

We may begin our inquiry with the celebrated case of *Raffles v. Wichelhaus*[85] which, it may be, is to the ordinary run of case law as the recently popular theatre of the absurd is to the ordinary run of theatre. Appropriately enough, even the report of the case is weird. It starts with a fairly detailed résumé of the pleadings, continues with a colloquy between losing counsel and two of the three judges who made up the court, gives the argument of the winning counsel who, after two sentences was "stopped by the Court" which, giving no reasons, abruptly announced: "There must be judgment for the defendants."

According to the declaration (or complaint) there was a contract for the sale of 125 bales of cotton to be shipped from Bombay and delivered at the dock in Liverpool. The contract term was that the cotton was "to arrive ex Peerless from Bombay"—"Peerless" being the name of the carrying ship. The plaintiff (seller) alleged that the cotton had arrived in Liverpool on the Peerless which had sailed from Bombay, that he had offered to deliver the cotton and that the defendant had breached the contract by refusing to accept or pay for it. The defendant's plea did not deny any of the allegations but stated that the Peerless which the defendant "meant and intended" was a ship which had sailed from Bombay in October (on which the plaintiff had shipped no cotton) and that the ship on which the plaintiff's cotton arrived "was another and different ship, which was also called the Peerless, and which sailed from Bombay, to wit, in December."

At that point there was a joinder in demurrer. As a piece of trial strategy, the decision of plaintiff's counsel to demur to the plea—thus conceding that the defendant meant to contract for goods to be carried on the October Peerless and not for the goods actually carried on the December Peerless —seems as mystifying as it proved to be mistaken. No doubt his thought was that, even with that concession, his client's case was overwhelming—and, from the point of view of a commercial lawyer, there was (and is) much to be said in favor of that position. Counsel had the bad luck, however, to come up against a trio of judges who were apparently incapable of understanding the fairly simple point which he tried, unavailingly, to make.[86]

Presumably the buyer's real reason for rejecting the cotton was that, at the time of tender, the Liverpool market price had fallen below the contract price of 17½d. per pound.[87] The fact that the buyer's Peerless had sailed from Bombay two months before the seller's Peerless suggests the possibility that the ship which sailed first also arrived first and that the market price had broken between the two arrival dates. In that case, it could be argued, the buyer had indeed suffered loss because of the seller's choice of the later ship. If that had been the case, however, the buyer would presumably have pleaded those facts, which would obviously have strengthened his case. In any event it does not necessarily follow that a ship sailing from Bombay in October would have made port in Liverpool before a ship sailing in December. Either Peerless may have been a sailing vessel, subject to the vagaries of wind and weather—or both of them may have been—and either one (or both) may have called at intermediate ports. Since the buyer did not in his plea raise any issue about the time of the seller's tender in Liverpool, we may, I think, safely assume that there was no such issue to be raised. Furthermore, as Milward (plaintiff's counsel) correctly pointed out, there was no provision in the contract relating to the time of sailing from Bombay.

The "fairly simple" point which Milward tried to make was that, under the contract term "to arrive ex Peerless," "it was immaterial by what ship the cotton was to arrive, so that it was a ship called the Peerless" and that the term meant only that "if the vessel is lost on the voyage, the contract is to be at an end" (that is, the seller would bear the loss but the buyer would have no claim for damages for non-delivery). In commercial understanding, that is exactly what the terms mean today and there is no reason to believe that they meant anything else a hundred years ago.[88] In technical language, Milward's argument was that the identity of the carrying ship was not a true condition of the contract. Thus, even on the assumption that the buyer had meant the October Peerless (and that his meaning was entitled to prevail), he would not have been justified in rejecting the tender of the cotton which arrived on the December Peerless. For mistake to justify rescission of a contract the mistake must relate to some fundamental aspect of the contractual performance; it was, as Milward said, given the commercial meaning of the contract term and the fact that no issue relating to the time of tender was raised, "immaterial" on which Peerless the cotton arrived.

Milward got absolutely nowhere in explaining this point to the court. Two of the judges, Pollock and Martin, kept interrupting him with questions which suggest that they had no idea what he was talking about. Their evident assumption was that if the contract said Peerless, then Peerless was a fundamental term (or condition) of the contract and Milward could go on talking until he was blue in the face without shaking them. There seems to be an air of increasing desperation in Milward's attempts to deal with the wooly-headed questions from the bench. Toward the end of his argument, perhaps distracted, he suddenly switched to an obviously unsound line: that parol evidence was not admissable to show which Peerless was meant—a diversionary tactic which the Court treated with the silent contempt it deserved.

Mellish, as counsel for the buyer, answered Milward. His first sentence effectively demolished Milward's unfortunate attempt to drag in the parol evidence rule. His second sentence was:

> That being so [i.e. the parol evidence being admissable], there was no consensus as idem, and therefore no binding contract.[89]

At that point he was stopped by the Court which forthwith announced judgment for Mellish's client.

There are really only two things we can make out of this curious case. One is that the judges, no doubt mistakenly, believed that the identity of the carrying ship was important—a true condition of the contract. The other is that they seem to have been immediately convinced by Mellish's consensus ad idem argument—that if buyer "meant" the October Peerless while seller "meant" the December Peerless (which was admitted by the demurrer), then there could be no contract since their minds had never met. None of the judges thought of asking Mellish what would seem to be obvious questions. Would a reasonably well-informed cotton merchant in Liverpool have known that there were two ships called Peerless? Ought this buyer to have known? If in fact the October Peerless had arrived in Liverpool first, had the buyer protested the seller's failure to tender the cotton? The failure of the judges, who had given Milward such a hard time, to put any questions to Mellish suggests that they were entirely content to let the case go off on the purely subjective failure of the minds to meet at the time the contract was entered into.

If *Raffles v. Wichelhaus* was the only exhibit to prove that the courts, well past the mid-point of the nineteenth century, were approaching the problem of formation of contract from a purely subjectionist point of view, we would not have got very far. There is, however, no dearth of other supporting exhibits. *Dickinson v. Dodds*, decided twelve years after *Raffles*, shows the same subjective theory being applied to the issue of the revocability of offers.[90] There was indeed a transatlantic analogue to *Raffles* in which the Massachusetts court came out exactly the same way the English court had and put the result expressly on the ground that the minds of the parties had not met.[91] There is another pair of transatlantic twins in which an English court and the Massachusetts court dealt with the situation in which A orders goods from B and which are in fact sold and delivered to him by C. In both cases A, on discovering C's identity, refused to pay for the goods, although he had accepted and used them without complaint and made no offer to return them. In the Massachusetts case, at least, return of the goods, which consisted of a year's supply of ice, would hardly have been feasible. In both cases, in seller's actions for the price, judgment went for the lucky buyers.[92] Here again, I suggest, we are in the presence of two of the finest flowers of nineteenth century subjectivism—an attitude which modulates smoothly into a theory of the untrammeled autonomy of the individual will and thence into the idea of unrestricted freedom of contract which was surely one of the master concepts of nineteenth century thought.

My principal reason for focusing our discussion on *Raffles v. Wichelhaus* is that Holmes has left us an altogether astonishing explanation of the true meaning of the case. In the lecture on Void and Voidable Contracts in *The Common Law* he stated the facts of the case and continued:

> It is commonly said that such a contract is void, because of mutual mistake as to the subject matter, and because therefore the parties did not consent to the same thing. But this way of putting it seems to me misleading. The law has nothing to do with the actual state of the parties' minds. In contract, as elsewhere, it must go by externals, and judge parties by their conduct. If there had been but one "Peerless," and the defendant had said "Peerless" by mistake, meaning "Peri," he would have been bound.[93] The true ground of the decision was not that each party meant a different thing from the other, as is implied by the explanation which has been mentioned, but that each said a different thing. The plaintiff offered one thing, the defendant expressed his assent to another.[94]

Even for Holmes this was an extraordinary tour de force. In the preceding lecture we observed at considerable length the process of "reinterpretation" to which the "leading cases" were subjected before being admitted to the pantheon.[95] The magician who could "objectify" *Raffles v. Wichelhaus* (to say nothing of *Kyle v. Kavanaugh*) could, the need arising, objectify anything. But why bother?

45

The central tenet of Holmes's jurisprudential thought was that the inevitable process of legal development was *from* a starting point at which rules of law are based on or derived from judgments about subjective moral fault or culpability *toward* an end point at which the original moral content of a given rule will have quite disappeared and the subjective state of mind of the defendant will have become irrelevant. The law moved from "subjective" to "objective," from "internal" to "external," from "informal" to "formal."[96] The successive lectures in *The Common Law* are designed as illustrations of how this developmental process has worked itself out in such fields as criminal law, torts, property and contracts. The process is more obvious, visible and thus easier to follow in criminal law and torts (which he took up first in his lectures) but, according to Holmes, is equally present across the entire spectrum of the common law. Thus it comes as no great surprise to the Holmesian adept to discover that the "actual state of the parties' minds" in *Raffles v. Wichelhaus* was irrelevant and that, despite popular misconceptions, the "true ground of the decision" was not that the parties "meant" different things but that they "said" different things.

Thus Holmes was willing to accept *Raffles* as a correctly decided case but insisted that it must be explained "objectively." Now, if you accept the result of a case, what difference does it make how you explain the result? In this context I think that it makes a good deal of difference. If ("in contract, as elsewhere") the "actual state of the parties' minds" is relevant, then each litigated case must become an extended factual inquiry into what was "intended," "meant," "believed" and so on. If, however, we can restrict ourselves to the "externals" (what the parties "said" or "did"), then the factual inquiry will be much simplified and in time can be dispensed with altogether as the courts accumulate precedents about recurring types of permissible and impermissible "conduct." By this process questions, originally perceived as questions of fact, will resolve themselves into questions of law. Broadly conceived, the Holmesian version of consideration theory is the classical illustration of this approach: questions of "fairness," "good faith," "duress," "fraud" and the like are all dealt with as questions of law under one or another of the aspects of the bargain theory of consideration. The objectification of *Raffles* points the way toward doing the same thing across the vague and cloudy area of "mistake."

In the preceding lecture I characterized the newly reformulated bargain theory of consideration as "the balance-wheel of the great machine" of the classical or general theory of contract. On a higher jurisprudential level the "objective theory of contract" became the great metaphysical solvent —the critical test for distinguishing between the false and the true. In the elaboration of consideration theory much wit and learning was devoted to the game, originally popularized by Holmes, of pretending that bargain theory was not only philosophically, economically and socially sound but that it also had the sanction of history. However the post-Holmesian "objectivists," led by Williston, make no attempt to argue that their principle had any common law past. Perhaps the attempt would have overtaxed even their own very considerable ingenuity. On the contrary, the emergence and triumph of the "objective theory" was put forward as one of the great accomplishments of recent times—the apprehension of a fundamental truth which had long been hidden in a deep morass of error.

Thus Williston:

> Doubtless the law is generally expressed in terms of subjective assent, rather than of objective expressions, the latter being said to be "evidence" of the former, as, for example, in the so-called parol evidence rule; but when it is established that this is no rule of evidence but rather a rule of substantive law, the whole subjective theory which is sometimes rather ludicrously epitomized by the quaintly archaic expression "meeting of the minds," falls to the ground.
>
> Under the guise of conclusive presumptions of mental assent from external acts, the law has been so built up that it can be expressed accurately only by saying that the elements requisite for the formation of a contract are exclusively external. . . .
>
> Thus . . . it is clear that the great majority of courts have discarded the impractical and unrealistic subjective standard (using the cliche "meeting of the minds") which seemed so appropriate and fitting a century or more ago in favor of an objective approach based on the *external* manifestation of mutual assent.[97]

The effect of the application of the objective theory to such areas of the law as mistake was of course to narrow the range within which mistake could be successfully pleaded as a defense. That is, it is no longer enough that I was subjectively mistaken, even with respect to a fundamental term of the contract. To get out of my contract (or to be successful in arguing that no contract was ever formed) I must show that my mistake was justifiable or excusable in the light of the generally accepted standards of the community. Just as the Holmesian formulation of consideration had exploded "the vulgar error that any benefit or any detriment would do" as a consideration to support a contract,[98] so the "objectification" of the mistake cases exploded the equally vulgar error that any mistake (or failure of the "minds" to "meet") would do as an escape from contractual liability. Now there are "mistakes" and "mistakes" and only some of them will do. With the narrowing of the range of availability of such excuses as mistake,[99] we move toward the ideal of absolute liability which, as has been noted earlier, was one of the basic ideas of the great theory.[100]

No legal system has ever carried into practice a theory of absolute contractual liability. Our own system, during the nineteenth century, may be the only one which has ever proclaimed such a theory. The proclamation was made in this country long before Holmes came on the scene and, at least in this country, was steadfastly adhered to, mostly as a matter of ritual incantation, throughout the century. The source of the absolute liability idea in English law was always confidently stated to be the seventeenth century case of *Paradine v. Jane*.[101] In that case, a landlord's action to recover rent, the tenant had pleaded that he should be excused from payment because, during the term of the lease, he had been evicted from the land by a royalist army under the command of Prince Rupert. The plea was held bad: "Though the whole army had been alien enemies, yet he ought to pay his rent."[102] Two hundred years later we find Morton, J., for the Massachusetts court, explaining the "general rule" on excuse by reason of impossibility in this fashion:

> [W]here the law imposes a duty upon anyone, inevitable accident may excuse the non-performance; for the law will not require of a party what, without any fault of his, he becomes unable to perform. But where the party by his agreement voluntarily assumes or creates a duty or charge upon himself, he shall be bound by his contract, and the nonperformance of it will not be excused by accident or inevitable necessity; for if he desired any such exception, he should have provided for it in his contract.[103]

This language was copied, almost word for word, from one of the seventeenth century reports of *Paradine v. Jane*[104]—a case which, in all probability, Judge Morton had never read and which he did not cite.

The story of the transmission of the *Paradine v. Jane* language from mid-seventeenth century England to mid-nineteenth century America is one of the curiosities of the legal literature. In its own day *Paradine* does not seem to have been a particularly celebrated case, nor does its seventeenth century meaning, so far as we can determine it, necessarily have much or anything to do with what came to be its nineteenth century meaning. One possibility is that the seventeenth century court meant merely that the tenant could not interpose his plea in the landlord's action for the rent but could bring an independent action against the landlord to recover whatever damages he had suffered as the result of his eviction by Prince Rupert; indeed, *Paradine* is cited to that proposition in a case decided in 1723.[105] Another possibility is that the court looked on the leasehold as a fully executed transaction, with the tenant bearing the risk of eviction in the same way that a buyer of chattels would bear the risk of their loss or destruction after receiving delivery of them from the seller.[106] The modern vogue of *Paradine* dates from Serjeant Williams's edition, first published in 1802, of Saunders, which was a collection of late seventeenth century cases. One of the cases in Saunders, *Walton v. Waterhouse*,[107] involved a covenant by a tenant to rebuild after a fire. In a lengthy note to *Walton v. Waterhouse*, Williams paraphrased the language used in the Aleyn report of *Paradine* and it was Williams's note which Judge Morton, in the Massachusetts case just referred to, cited and copied out. Indeed, there are several early nineteenth century references to *Paradine v. Jane* which assume that the case, given the context in which Williams had put it, involved a tenant's covenant to rebuild.[108]

However, all this is mere bibliographical amusement. The importance of the story lies in the facts that the Williams edition of Saunders was highly successful—having been many times reprinted both in England and in the United States—and that the Note to *Walton v. Waterhouse* became celebrated—the apparent meaning of the Note being that English law for two hundred years past had steadfastly adhered to a theory of absolute contractual liability.[109] Such a theory evidently made sense to the judges—particularly the American judges—of a hundred years and more ago. It would take us too far afield to inquire into the reasons for the success of such a theory; we might perhaps speculate that the Puritan ethic was somehow involved. The moral fervor with which the nineteenth century judges continued to recite the formula that not even "accident or inevitable necessity" will excuse the non-performance of a duty voluntarily assumed is reminiscent of the moral fervor which the same judges brought to their statement of the formula that a plaintiff who is himself in willful or substantial default in his contractual performance can never recover anything, even for benefits which he may, by a partial performance, have conferred on the defendant and which the defendant retains.[110] Let me repeat a point I have already made: the absolute liability idea was often preached but rarely practiced —indeed, much the same thing can be said of the plaintiff in default idea. This comment makes the ideas themselves no less significant; it is always a matter of the highest interest when the courts—like people generally—say one thing while doing its opposite. But we can defer until a later point our discussion of how the courts avoided practicing on weekdays what they so eloquently preached on Sundays.

The absolute liability idea was enthusiastically picked up and incorporated into the structure by the artisans of the great theory. At first blush this may appear surprising, if it is true, as I have suggested, that the essential thrust of the theory was to confine liability within the narrowest possible limits. If that is so, why not make it difficult to get into a contract in the first place (under the reformulated consideration theory) but easy to get out (under a broad theory of excuse)? We are faced, however, with the fact that the nineteenth century theorists embraced both a narrow consideration theory and a narrow excuse theory, as well as with the fact that, in our own century, the breakdown of nineteenth century consideration theory has been paralleled by a breakdown of nineteenth century absolute liability theory. Evidently a free and easy approach to the problem of contract formation goes hand in hand with a free and easy approach to the problem of contract dissolution or excuse—and vice versa. Absolute liability also fitted into an aspect of the objective theory of contract which we have earlier commented on. That is, questions of fact were, so far as possible, avoided or, where they could not be avoided, were rephrased as questions of law. To the extent that a theory of excuse from a contractual obligation is admitted, it becomes necessary to take particular factual situations into account. What "accident," what "inevitable necessity," what change of circumstance, what mistake will excuse? Such factual inquiry is neatly avoided by the proclamation that liability is absolute; if a "duty or charge voluntarily assumed" is never discharged, though the heavens fall, that is obviously, the end of the matter. And, consistently with its acceptance of the idea of absolute liability, the theory discouraged any further case law development of excuse by reason of fraud, duress, coercion, and the like.[111] In this context we will do well to recall Holmes's comment that: "The whole doctrine of contract is formal and external."[112]

The absolute liability idea was put forward in double harness with the idea that contract damages were to be kept low and were to be sharply differentiated from tort damages. Indeed, a restrictive approach toward damage recovery seems a necessary component of any idea of absolute liability—even one that was meant to be honored more in the breach than in the observance.

Since 1854 the starting point for all discussion of contract damage theory has been *Hadley v. Baxendale*[113]—although why such an essentially uninteresting case, decided in a not very good opinion by a judge otherwise unknown to fame, should immediately have become celebrated on both sides of the Atlantic is one of the mysteries of legal history. Plaintiffs were owners of a mill which had been shut down because of a broken crankshaft. Defendants were common carriers who had been engaged to transport the broken crankshaft to Greenwich where it was to be used by the manufacturer as a "pattern" for the new crankshaft. Delivery of the old crankshaft to the manufacturer was delayed by the carrier's negligence; wherefore the mill was shut down for several days longer than it would otherwise have been. Plaintiffs sued to recover the profits lost by the mill during the period of delay. There was a jury verdict for the plaintiffs in the amount of £25,[114] which was reversed in the Court of Exchequer.

Baron Alderson's opinion in *Hadley* stated as a general rule that the damages recoverable for breach of contract were

such as may fairly and reasonably be considered either arising naturally, i.e. according to the usual course of things,

54

from such breach of contract itself, or such as may reasonably be supposed to have been in the contemplation of both parties, at the time they made the contract, as the probable result of the breach of it.

If, he went on, there were "special circumstances" which took the case out of "the usual course of things," such special circumstances had to be communicated to the defendant at the time he entered into the contract. The assumption is that the "special circumstances," once communicated to the defendant, would be within his "contemplation" so that, on breach, he would be liable for the "special" damages. The fact that the only reason for the mill's being shut down was the broken crankshaft amounted to "special circumstances." However, all that had been communicated to the defendants, according to Alderson, was that they were taking the broken crankshaft of a mill back to the manufacturer.[115] It did not necessarily follow that they were to be charged with the knowledge that the mill was shut down because of the broken crankshaft and would have to remain shut down until the new crankshaft came back from Greenwich. The mill might have been equipped with a spare crankshaft—in which case it would not have been shut down at all, unless, of course, the spare broke too—or as another alternative, the mill might have been shut down for reasons which had nothing to do with the crankshaft. Since there had been insufficient communication of the "special circumstances," the plaintiffs were not entitled to recover their lost profits.

In the hundred odd years since the case was decided, the

compendious formula of *Hadley v. Baxendale* has meant all things to all men. We are presently concerned with the late nineteenth century reaction to Baron Alderson's "rule"—a reaction which was distinctly hostile on the ground that Alderson had gone much too far in the direction of allowing recovery of what came to be called "special" or "consequential" damages. Thus Holmes:

> If a breach of contract were regarded in the same light as a tort, it would seem that if, in the course of performance of the contract the promisor should be notified of any particular consequence which would result from its not being performed, he should be held liable for that consequence in the event of non-performance. Such a suggestion has been made. But it has not been accepted as the law. On the contrary, according to the opinion of a very able judge, which seems to be generally followed, notice even at the time of making the contract, of special circumstances out of which special damages would arise in case of breach, is not sufficient unless the assumption of that risk is to be taken as having fairly entered into the contract. If a carrier should undertake to carry the machinery of a sawmill from Liverpool to Vancouver's Island, and should fail to do so, he probably would not be held liable for the rate of hire of such machinery during the necessary delay, although he might know that it could not be replaced without sending to England, unless he was fairly understood to accept "the contract with the special condition attached to it."[116]

Historically, Holmes and other critics[117] of the *Hadley*

formulation had a good deal on their side. We are accustomed to take as dogma the idea that contract damages should be "compensatory"—no more but certainly no less—and that what has come to be called the "expectation interest"—that is, anticipated profits—is one of the interests, perhaps the principal interest, to be protected. In fact, several damage rules relating to particular types of contracts had become established during the pre-*Hadley* period—that is, during the first half of the nineteenth century, which is far back as judicially elaborated contract damage theory goes. (The growth of damage theory is, thus, contemporaneous with the growth of the several commercial law specialties—Justice Story's "commercial contracts"[118]—and may be ascribed to the same underlying cause.) The pre-*Hadley* damage rules shared the common feature that none of them protected the expectation interest or opened to admit special or consequential damages. The rule of *Flureau v. Thornhill*[119] restricted vendee's damages for seller's breach of a land contract by failure to make good title to what we would call the vendee's reliance expenses—searching title and so on. The rule on damages for breach of contracts to lend or pay money restricted damages to any excess interest which the promisee might have to pay to get the money from another source—the underlying assumption being, evidently, that money is universally and instantly available.[120] The rule on damages for breach of contract to sell goods restricted the damages to whatever differential there might be between the contract price of the goods and their market price at the time and place of delivery.[121] Indeed, in the course of his *Hadley* opinion Baron Alderson referred to the first two of these rules, observing that such "conventional rules," as he called them, will prevail over his own "general rule" "because . . . both parties may reasonably be presumed to contemplate the estimation of the amount of damages according to the conventional rule." Thus the essential novelty of the *Hadley* formula, it may be suggested, was its affirmative statement that, subject to the limitation of foreseeability and provided only that all the "special circumstances" were communicated, lost profits and other consequential damages caused by breach of a contractual duty were recoverable.[122]

In the nineteenth century reaction, it was this affirmative aspect of the *Hadley* rule that came under attack as going much too far and as not sufficiently preserving the differentiation between contract and tort.[123] In the Holmesian revision foreseeability was not enough; there must have been a deliberate and conscious assumption of the risk by the contract-breaker—and it is worth recalling, in this context, Holmes's insistence that it made not a particle of difference whether a contract was breached with malicious intent or with the purest of motives.[124] In addition to the "assumption of risk" limitation on the *Hadley* rule, much stress was also laid on the limitations that were built into the rule itself. "Forseeability" and "communication" are, evidently, manipulable concepts. During the period of the reaction they were manipulated, with great sophistication, in favor of defendants and against plaintiffs seeking large damage awards.[125] While *Hadley* itself was being thus restrictively construed, the pre-*Hadley* damage formulae—Baron

Alderson's "conventional rules"—flourished as never before. For a plaintiff to escape from the contract and market rule in a sales case seemed to be an accomplishment on the same order of difficulty as a rich man's entrance into heaven.

We have now completed our guided tour of the quaint old general theory of contract, commenting as we went on such of the ruins as are still identifiable. What happened to the great structure—and why—will be the subject of the following lecture.

III

Decline and Fall

THE FIRST POINT to be made is that the general theory of contract was never as neat and tidy and all-of-a-piece in the real world as it was made to appear in casebook and treatise and Restatement (although we shall have more to say about Restatements presently). The apparent unity of doctrine was achieved through what might be called an extremely selective handling of the case material. This achievement was, of course, immensely facilitated by the custom, initiated by Langdell, of relying to an extraordinary degree on English cases as authoritative precedents.[126] It is true that English case law, on any given point, presents a more unified appearance than does our own case law. There are fewer cases—the English have long adhered to the wise practice of reporting only some of their cases, not all of them as we have done since the West Publishing Company went into the business in the 1880s—and the cases proceed from a unitary court system that leads up to a court of last resort which, until a few years ago, declared that it lacked power to reverse any of its own prior decisions.[127] English case law is manageable in a way that American case law has never been. In the preceding lectures I have described some of the ways in which the American commentators, in effect, "managed" the English cases. We need not accuse Langdell and his successors of an unbecoming Anglophilism; for the structure they wanted to build, the English cases were the best—indeed the only possible—building materials. Cases from a few Eastern jurisdictions could, occasionally, be put to use. What was going on in such remote, out-of-the-way places as Ohio and Wisconsin and North Dakota could —indeed, if the appearance of unity was to be maintained, had to be—disregarded.

We are only gradually coming to realize how much diversity was, for a considerable period, successfully concealed. Professor Lon Fuller, in his remarkable article on The Reliance Interest in Contract Damages (1936), pointed out that the courts had in fact been protecting what he christened the "reliance interest" to a much greater degree than had been assumed.[128] In much the same way, Professor Friedrich Kessler, in his equally remarkable article on Bargaining in Good Faith and Freedom of Contract (1964), has drawn our attention to the considerable number of instances in which courts have imposed what might be called a pre-contractual duty to bargain in good faith—a principle whose very existence in Anglo-American jurisprudence has been denied, doubted or simply ignored.[129] Such case law undergrounds as these are instructive from more than one point of view. Until some scholar has discovered their existence and reported on them in the respectable pages of the *Harvard Law Review* or the *Yale Law Journal,* no one knows of them. Such cases do not fit into the received categories; consequently they do not fit into the key-number system of the digests; consequently, until a Fuller or a Kessler comes along, no one can find them even if he goes looking for them. Indeed, most of the time, it turns out that courts which decide such underground cases are apparently unaware that there are any other cases of the sort. We might call this process the jurisprudence of instinct or, perhaps, of ignorance. That judicial ignorance is one of the great motivating forces of law reform has, of course, long been an open secret.[130]

On its own terms, however, the theory of contract, as formulated by Holmes and Williston, seems to have gone into its protracted period of breakdown almost from the moment of its birth. I have credited Holmes and Williston with the design and execution of the great theory. It is tempting to set Cardozo and Corbin over against them as the engineers of its destruction. Tempting and by no means untrue. Cardozo's attack was subtle, evasive, hesitant—it is by no means easy to know how far that master of judicial ambiguity meant us to go with the cryptic hints which he provided for our delectation and bewilderment. But it is certain that the outlines of the law of contract that emerged from the opinions of the New York Court of Appeals during the period of Cardozo's dominance of that court had little enough to do with the law of contract as it was taught at Harvard during the same period. Corbin's attack was more forthright. We are apt to think of Corbin as having been more an Establishment figure than in fact he was. The reason for that misjudgment is that his treatise on Contracts—which I will describe as the greatest law book ever written—bears the publication date: 1950. It is true that, by 1950, the ideas and the reforms which Corbin argued for were no longer particularly novel; the ideas had been the mother's milk of beginning law students for a generation or more and most of the reforms had long since been accomplished. We forget that Corbin—perhaps unwisely—had spent the better part of fifty years readying the treatise for publication. This is, despite the publication date, a book conceived in 1910 or thereabouts, the main lines of which had no doubt been thrown down by 1920. We can trace many of the ideas back into Corbin's early articles; from what we know of the process of aging, there can be no doubt that all the main ideas of the treatise had been formulated by the time of World War I. So resituated in time, Corbin's attack on the prevailing orthodoxy assumes revolutionary proportions.

Corbin's abiding interest was in what he called the "operative facts" of cases; he had no love for, indeed little patience with, doctrine. He remarked, toward the beginning of his discussion of consideration:

> [A] sufficient reason for comparative historical study of cases in great number is the fact that such study frees the teacher and the lawyer and the judge from the illusion of certainty; and from the delusion that law is absolute and eternal, that doctrines can be used mechanically, and that there are correct and unchangeable definitions.[131]

Evidently we have entered a universe of discourse which simply has no meeting point with the Holmesian universe in which the doctrine of contract was, and was meant to be, "wholly formal and external."[132] Indeed Corbin's entire discussion of consideration theory is essentially a demonstration that the Holmesian model was wrong—wrong as a matter of historical fact (which, of course, it was) and also wrong as a matter of social policy (which is a different question entirely).

We must now deal with the mysterious episode of the Restatements. Why on earth, in the early 1920s, should the project of "restating" the common law have seemed necessary, desirable or even sensible to the eminent group of lawyers, judges and scholars who undertook the task and worked at it devotedly over many years? I have suggested elsewhere that the Restatement project can be taken as the almost instinctive reaction of the legal establishment of the time to the attack of the so-called legal realists.[133] What the realists had principally attacked, savagely and successfully, was the essentially Langdellian idea that cases can be arranged to make sense—indeed scientific sense. Such an idea, the realists demonstrated, was purest moonshine and nonsense. By the 1930s, at least in the law schools, the Langdellian position had become untenable—and, in an unkind reversal, the case method of teaching had been turned on its head and used to disprove everything its inventor had held dear. But in the 1920s there was still hope that the revolution could be put down, that unity of doctrine could be maintained and that an essentially pure case law system could be preserved from further statutory encroachment. The radical solution to the breakdown of the case law system, which the realists had perceived, would, no doubt, have been statutes all around—a universal, Benthamite codification. The conservative response, which, looked on as a delaying action, was remarkably successful, was the provision of Restatements of Contracts, Torts, Property and the like.

Williston and Corbin were unquestionably the dominant intellectual influences in the drafting of the *Restatement of Contracts*—Williston as Chief Reporter and Corbin as his principal assistant. No doubt it was their joint participation which insured the extraordinarily high technical quality of the product: the *Restatement of Contracts* is not only the best of the Restatements, it is one of the great legal accomplishments of all time. No doubt it was also their joint participation—bearing in mind that Williston and Corbin held antithetical points of view on almost every conceivable point of law—that accounts for the schizophrenic quality which makes the *Restatement*, viewed historically, the fascinating document which it is.[134]

If Corbin was, as I have characterized him, a nonestablishment revolutionary, the question legitimately arises: What was he doing as part of the Restatement crew? Why was he not outside on the barricades leading the revolutionary troops with Llewellyn, perhaps, as his principal aide? I simply do not know the answer to the question. Chronologically, Corbin belonged to an in-between generation—he came after the Willistons and before the Llewellyns. He and Williston, despite the difference in their ages, temperaments and theoretical approaches, maintained a close and affectionate friendship throughout most of their long lifetimes. Corbin never quite joined the realist movement—although Llewellyn looked on Corbin as his "father in the law." Perhaps in the 1920s Corbin felt that he could accomplish more working from a base within the establishment than he could working from outside with those with whom he was, undoubtedly, more closely allied, both tempermentally and doctrinally.

I have referred to the Restatement's schizophrenia. It is time to give chapter and verse. The first lesson will be the *Restatement's* definition of consideration (§ 75) taken in connection with its most celebrated section—§ 90, captioned Promise Reasonably Inducing Definite and Substantial Action.

First § 75:

> (1)   Consideration for a promise is
>
> (a) an act other than a promise, or
> (b) a forbearance, or
> (c) the creation, modification or destruction of a legal relation, or
> (d) a return promise,
> bargained for and given in exchange for the promise.
>
> (2)   Consideration may be given to the promisor or to some other person. It may be given by the promisee or by some other person.

This is, of course, pure Holmes. The venerable Justice took no part in the Restatement project. It is unlikely that he ever looked at the *Restatement of Contracts.* If, however, § 75 was ever drawn to his attention, it is not hard to imagine him chuckling at the thought of how his revolutionary teaching of the 1880s had become the orthodoxy of a half-century later.

Now § 90:

A promise which the promisor should reasonably expect to induce action or forbearance of a definite and substantial character on the part of the promisee and which does induce such action or forbearance is binding if injustice can be avoided only by enforcement of the promise.

And what is that all about? We have become accustomed to the idea, without in the least understanding it, that the universe includes both matter and anti-matter. Perhaps what we have here is Restatement and anti-Restatement or Contract and anti-Contract. We can be sure that Holmes, who relished a good paradox, would have laughed aloud at the sequence of § 75 and § 90. The one thing that is clear is that these two contradictory propositions cannot live comfortably together: in the end one must swallow the other up.

A good many years ago Professor Corbin gave me his version of how this unlikely combination came about.[135] When the Restaters and their advisors came to the definition of consideration, Williston proposed in substance what became § 75. Corbin submitted a quite different proposal. To understand what the Corbin proposal was about, it is necessary to backtrack somewhat. Even after the Holmesian or bargain theory of consideration had won all but universal acceptance, the New York Court of Appeals had, during the Cardozo period, pursued a line of its own. There is a long series of Cardozo contract opinions, scattered over his long tenure on that court.[136] Taken all in all, they express what might be called an expansive theory of contract. Courts should make contracts wherever possible, rather than the other way around.[137] Missing terms can be supplied.[138] If an express promise is lacking, an implied promise can easily be found.[139] In particular Cardozo delighted in weaving gossamer spider webs of consideration. There was consideration for a father's promise to pay his engaged daughter an annuity after marriage in the fact that the engaged couple, instead of breaking off the engagement, had in fact married.[140] There was consideration for a pledge to a college endowment campaign (which the donor had later sought to revoke) in the fact that the college, by accepting the pledge, had come under an implied duty to memoralize the donor's name: "The longing for posthumous remembrance is an emotion not so weak as to justify us in saying that its gratification is a negligible good."[141] Evidently a judge who could find "consideration" in *DeCicco v. Schweizer* or in the *Allegheny College* case could, when he was so inclined, find consideration anywhere: the term had been so broadened as to have become meaningless. We may now return to the Restatement debate on the consideration definition. Corbin, who had been deeply influenced by Cardozo, proposed to the Restaters what might be called a Cardozoean definition of consideration—broad, vague and, essentially, meaningless—a common law equivalent of causa, or cause.[142] In the debate Corbin and the Cardozoeans lost out to Williston and the Holmesians. In Williston's view, that should have been the end of the matter.

Instead, Corbin returned to the attack. At the next meeting of the Restatement group, he addressed them more or less in the following manner: Gentlemen, you are engaged in restating the common law of contracts. You have recently adopted a definition of consideration. I now submit to you a list of cases—hundreds, perhaps or thousands?—in which courts have imposed contractual liability under circumstances in which, according to your definition, there would be no consideration and therefore no liability. Gentlemen, what do you intend to do about these cases?

To understand Corbin's point we must backtrack and digress again. I have made the point that Holmesian consideration theory had, as Holmes perfectly well knew, not so much as a leg to stand on if the matter is taken historically.[143] Going back into the past, there was an indefinite number of cases which had imposed liability, in the name of consideration, where nothing like Holmes's "reciprocal conventional inducement"[144] was anywhere in sight. Holmes's point was that these were bad cases and that the range of contractual liability should be confined within narrower limits. By the turn of the century, except in New York, the strict bargain theory of consideration had won general acceptance. But, unlike Holmes, many judges, it appeared, were not prepared to look with stony-eyed indifference on the plight of a plaintiff who had, to his detriment, relied on a defendant's assurances without the protection of a formal contract. However, the new doctrine precluded the judges of the 1900 crop from saying, as their predecessors would have said a half-century earlier, that the "detriment" itself was "consideration." They had to find a new solution, or, at least, a new terminology. In such a situation the word that comes instinctively to the mind of any judge is, of course, "estoppel"—which is simply a way of saying that, for reasons which the court does not care to discuss, there must be judgment for plaintiff. And in the contract cases after 1900 the word "estoppel," modulating into such phrases as "equitable estoppel" and "promissory estoppel," began to appear with increasing frequency.[145] Thus Corbin, in his submission to the Restaters, was plentifully supplied with new, as well as with old, case material.[146]

The Restaters, honorable men, evidently found Corbin's argument unanswerable. However, instead of reopening the debate on the consideration definition, they elected to stand by § 75 but to add a new section—§ 90—incorporating the estoppel idea although without using the word "estoppel." The extent to which the new section § 90 was to be allowed to undercut the underlying principle of § 75 was left entirely unresolved. The format of the Restatement included analytical, discursive, often lengthy comments, interspersed with illustrations—that is, hypothetical cases, the facts of which were frequently drawn from real cases. Section 90 is almost the only section of the *Restatement of Contracts* which has no Comment at all. Four hypothetical cases, none of them, so far as I know, based on a real case, are offered as "illustrations," presumably to indicate the range which the section was meant to have. An attentive study of the four illustrations will lead any analyst to the despairing conclusion, which is of course reinforced by the mysterious text of § 90 itself, that no one had any idea what the damn thing meant.[147]

For other illustrations of the pervading schizophrenia

of the *Restatement of Contracts*, I will refer to the *Restatement's* treatment of such matters as the following: third party beneficiaries, anticipatory breach, excuse by reason of impossibility or frustration, and whether a plaintiff who is himself in default can ever recover.[148] We need not go into any detail. For our purposes it is enough to say that the classical theory, no doubt effectively championed by Williston, strongly disapproved the doctrines of third-party beneficiaries and of anticipatory breach, was committed to a theory of absolute liability, and accepted the idea that plaintiffs in default should never recover. On most of these points Corbin, in his early writings, had taken the opposite position.[149] On each of them the *Restatement* came out curiously fudged or blurred, pointing equivocally in all directions at once. The *Restatement*, we might say, ended up uneasily poised between past and future, which is no doubt the best thing that could have been done.

The future, of course, won, as it always does. During the past forty years we have seen the effective dismantling of the formal system of classical contract theory. We have witnessed what it does not seem too farfetched to describe as an explosion of liability. The detail of the affair would be tedious, but a few descriptive generalizations are in order. In the preceding lectures I suggested that the essential features of the classical theory were the narrowing of the range of liability under the reformulated consideration theory, the acceptance, within those limits, of the idea of absolute liability, and a restrictive or negative approach toward the recovery of large damage awards. We may review what has been going on under these three heads.

Section 90 of the *Restatement* has borne strange fruit. (It may be remarked, parenthetically, that § 75 has not been heard of for some time.) In early judicial, and for that matter academic, discussions of § 90, there was a general assumption that the principle of § 90, however it should be described, should find its application mostly, if not entirely, in what might be called non-commercial situations. Judge Learned Hand once suggested that § 90, if it had any scope at all, which he was inclined to doubt, should be restricted to donative or gift promises.[150] Professionals should play the game according to the professional rules. If A, in a commercial context, made what could be described as an offer to B, then A's liability to B should depend on the formal rules of offer, acceptance and consideration and on nothing else. The course of decision has, however, seen a gradual expansion of § 90 as a principle of decision in a good many types of commercial situations.[151] Even more interestingly, some of the recent cases are beginning to suggest that liability under § 90 or the doctrine of promissory estoppel or however it is described is somehow different from liability in contract. Thus, it may be, defenses based on the statute of frauds or the contract statute of limitation or the parol evidence rule—all these being looked on as contract-based defenses—are no longer available if the underlying theory of liability—§ 90 or an analogue—is not contract theory at all.[152] This idea, if it spreads, could have interesting ramifications in the development of damage rules.[153]

Such case law developments are reflected in an altogether fascinating manner in the provisions of the so-called *Second Restatement of Contracts*. However, before we go on to an analysis of these provisions, I think we will do well to brood for a few minutes on the problem: Why should there be a second series of Restatements? In discussing the "mysterious episode" of what has turned out to be the first series of Restatements, I made the suggestion that the project could be taken as "the almost instinctive reaction of the legal establishment of the time to the attack of the so-called legal realists" and as a final desperate attempt to preserve "unity of doctrine" in an "essentially pure case law system."[154] There can be little or no doubt that the first generation of Restaters implicitly assumed that they were reducing to black letter text what we like to call the "fundamental principles of the common law." Now, we are all aware that rules of law change through time but many of us like to think that our "fundamental principles" are eternal and unchanging. As William Draper Lewis, the founder and Director of the American Law Institute, observed in his Introduction to the *Restatement of Contracts:* "The function of the courts is to decide the controversies brought before them. The function of the Institute [in preparing the Restatements] is to state clearly and precisely in the light of the decisions the principles and rules of the common law."[155] Thus the process was one of abstraction and induction: the underlying "principles" and "rules" were to be extracted from the existing mass of case law and stated (or restated) in a clear and precise fashion.[156] There would, of course, continue to be more cases, but it might be hoped— it obviously was hoped—that the "principles" and even the "rules," once they had been properly restated, would endure—if not forever, at least for a long time. All that being true, all that would be needed to keep the Restatements "up to date" would be periodic collections of new cases annotated to the relevant principles and rules; the Institute has indeed published such collections in a series of volumes entitled *The Restatements in the Courts*. In 1952, however, the decision seems to have been made that collecting cases was not enough and that a whole new series of Restatements was needed.[157] What happened to make the assumptions or illusions of the first generation of Restaters seem no longer tenable to their successors of the second generation?[158]

For one thing, no principles of law, or of anything else, can be guaranteed good past the next revolution. I dare say that no one will dispute the fact that, since the 1930s, there has been a world-wide revolution, scientific, social, economic and political. In some parts of the world the revolution has been accompanied by the violent overthrow of existing political regimes. In other parts of the world the same revolution has, so far, been accomplished without such an overthrow. One of the minor by-products of the revolution through which my own generation has lived will, of necessity, be the reformulation not merely of the specific "principles and rules of the common law" but of our basic attitudes toward the process of law itself. The members of the American Law Institute are not, as I once remarked in a quite different context, revolutionaries in their habits of thought or ways of living.[159] Nevertheless, those who live through such a period as our own will not escape the infection of the revolutionary virus, no matter how clearly they may see themselves as the continuers of the virtuous old ways. We may take the second series of Restatements as symbolizing that process of infection.

For another thing, the "essentially pure case law system" which the first Restaters hypothesized and instinctively sought to preserve[160] has not been preserved. Ironically, the American Law Institute itself became a party to the greatest breach which has so far been made in that system through its sponsorship of the Uniform Commercial Code.[161] The tide of codification continues to press heavily against the few remaining islands where the writ of the common law still runs and there can be little doubt that in another generation or two the change-over from an almost pure case law system to an almost pure statutory system will have been completed. The Restatements (Second) are in large part much less concerned with extracting from the cases the true "principles and rules of the common law" than they are with articulating the policy of the legislative reforms of the past thirty years or so. The original Restaters may have believed that they were working for all time; their successors do not seem to share that happy optimism.[162]

We may now observe some of the things that have been going on in the real world by taking note of what has happened to §§ 75 and 90 of *Restatement (First)* on the way to *Restatement (Second)*.[163]

Restatement (First) § 75 (Definition of Consideration)[164] has been somewhat rewritten but, so far as I can make out, has not been changed in substance in *Restatement (Second)* § 75 [§ 71]. The accompanying Comment has, however, been revised in such a way as to leave no doubt that we are now in an antithetical universe of discourse. The § 75 Comment in *Restatement (First)* began with an authentically Willistonian flourish:

> No duty is generally imposed on one who makes an informal promise unless the promise is supported by sufficient consideration. . . .

The lead to the § 75 [§ 71] Comment in *Restatement (Second)* introduces us to the sound of a much less certain trumpet:

> The word "consideration" has often been used with meanings different from that given here. It is often used merely to express the legal conclusion that a promise is enforceable.

The Comment, we might say, has been Corbinized.[165] The only recognition of the existence of § 90 in the *Restatement (First)* § 75 Comment was the somewhat grudging concession that "some informal promises are enforceable without the element of bargain. These fall and are placed in the category of contracts which are binding without assent or consideration (see §§ 85–94)."[166] Furthermore, Illustration 2 to § 75 in *Restatement (First)* hypothesized that "A promises B $500 when B goes to college" and concluded that "If the promise . . . is reasonably to be understood as a gratuity, payable on the stated contingency, B's going to college is not consideration for A's promise." The § 75 Illustration carried no cross-reference to § 90 where one of the Illustrations was to the effect that an apparently identical "if B goes to college" promise is "binding" on A.[167] The revised § 75 [§ 71] Comment in *Restatement (Second)* continues, properly enough, to emphasize the essentially Holmesian meaning of "bargain" theory.[168] However, the "when B goes to college" illustration has been dropped and the following new illustration substituted: "A promises to make a gift of $10 to B. In reliance on the promise B buys a book from C and promises to pay C $10 for it. There is no consideration for A's promise. As to the enforceability of such promises, see § 90." The attentive reader of the § 75 [§ 71] Commentary in *Restatement (Second)* will be in no danger of concluding, as the attentive reader of *Restatement (First)* might well have done, that § 75 contains the truth, the whole truth and nothing but the truth.

However, the Corbinization of § 75 is insignificant quite compared to what has happened to § 90. Original § 90, as I have pointed out, was exposed to the world naked of Comment and provided with four ambiguous illustrations as its sole capital.[169] Text and illustration together took up less than a page. Revised § 90 with its Comment and Illustrations runs to over twelve pages and the original four Illustrations have grown to seventeen.[170] A few minor changes have been made in the text of revised § 90: the original requirement that the promisee's action or forbearance be "of a definite and substantial character" has been deleted and a new sentence has been added which reads: "The remedy granted for breach may be limited as justice requires."[171] According to the Reporter's Notes these two changes are related—presumably in the sense that the "remedy granted" will be appropriately "limited" when the promisee's reliance fails to qualify as "definite and substantial."[172]

The principal change from *Restatement* (*First*) rests, however, in the elaborate Commentary which has been provided. The reliance principle, we are told, may have been, historically, the basis for "the enforcement of informal contracts in the action of assumpsit."

> Certainly [the Comment continues] reliance is one of the main bases for enforcement of the half-completed exchange, and the probability of reliance lends support to the enforcement of the executory exchange. . . . This Section thus states a basic principle which often renders inquiry unnecessary as to the precise scope of the policy of enforcing bargains.[173]

Thus the unwanted stepchild of *Restatement* (*First*) has become "a basic principle" of *Restatement* (*Second*) which, the comment seems to suggest, prevails, in case of need, over the competing "bargain theory" of § 75 [§ 71].[174] The Comment and the new Illustrations are entirely clear that the principle of § 90 is applicable in commercial contexts as well as in non-commercial ones—thus disposing of one of the suggested limitations on the use of original § 90.[175] No doubt wisely, the draftsman of the Comment refrains from taking any position on the suggestions in some recent cases that a § 90 recovery is not a contract recovery at all.[176]

Clearly enough the unresolved ambiguity in the relationship between § 75 and § 90 in the *Restatement* (*First*) has now been resolved in favor of the promissory estoppel principle of § 90 which has, in effect, swallowed up the bargain principle of § 75. The wholly executory exchange where neither party has yet taken any action would seem to be the only situation in which it would be necessary to look at § 75 —and even there, as the Comment somewhat mysteriously suggests, the "probability of reliance" may be a sufficient reason for enforcement without inquiring into whether or not there was any "consideration."

Originally the promissory estoppel idea was used to protect plaintiffs who had relied, to their own detriment but without conferring any benefit on the defendants, on pre-contractual or non-contractual representations. An even more compelling case for protection, it may be thought, is made by plaintiffs who have in fact conferred benefits on defendants who retain them. The "benefit conferred" idea can come up in situations which have nothing to do with contractual obligations voluntarily assumed. In a hypothetical case which comes down to us from Roman law, a stranger puts fertilizer on my land, as a result of which I am enabled to grow a bumper crop. Or a physician renders services to an unconscious man who dies without regaining consciousness. The idea also presents itself in contractual situations in which the plaintiff has partly performed his contractual obligation but has stopped short of complete performance, the defendant retaining the benefit of the part performance. An agricultural laborer, engaged for a year, quits after nine months. A builder leaves the house, which he has been building on the defendant's land, unfinished. Must I pay for the fertilizer? Must the dead man's estate pay the physician's bill? Must the employer pay for the nine months of labor which he received? Must the homeowner pay for what has been done on his house? The answer which classical contract theory gave to these questions was, of course: No. People who fertilize other people's land or play the good Samaritan are "officious intermeddlers"—volunteers whom even equity will not aid.[177] Plaintiffs who have defaulted on the complete performance of their contractual duty are entitled to recover nothing for what they have done.[178]

As we might expect, the refusal to give protection in the "benefit conferred" cases has been gradually suffering a reversal. The difficulty which the courts have had with such cases is, perhaps, reflected in the variety of explanations which have been offered to justify the plaintiff's recovery. The old variant of the common law action of assumpsit known as indebitatus assumpsit has been a useful crutch to explain why plaintiff recovers, not, of course, strictly in contract, but in quantum meruit.[179] More adventurous courts have turned to the idea of a "contract implied in law," a "quasi-contract"—not really a contract, a legal fiction necessary to promote the ends of justice and, in particular, to prevent "unjust enrichment."[180] Rules of "substantial performance" were developed to protect plaintiffs who had almost, but not quite, completed performance.[181] And reputable courts have even suggested that plaintiffs, conceded to be in willful and substantial default, should nevertheless recover the value of whatever it is they have conferred on the defendant.[182] The rejection of classical theory has thus been proceeding, albeit in a confused and sprawling pattern, on the benefit side as well as on the detriment side.

This uneven development is neatly caught for us in a new section which has been added to the *Restatement* (*Second*) as § 89A [§ 86] (Promise for Benefit Received). The

hesitant and cautious text of the new section no doubt reflects the uncertainties of the Reporter and his advisers:

(1)   A promise made in recognition of a benefit previously received by the promisor from the promisee is
binding to the extent necessary to prevent injustice.

(2)   A promise is not binding under Subsection (1)
(a) if the promisee conferred the benefit as a gift or
for other reasons the promisor has not been
unjustly enriched; or
(b) to the extent that its value is disproportionate to
the benefit.

This is far from going the whole hog on the unjust enrichment idea. For one thing, the ungrateful recipient may keep
whatever he has received without paying for it so long as he
is clever enough to avoid making a "promise" to repay. (Of
course courts which have learned how easy it is to imply
promises to make contracts could easily use the same technique in this context.) For another thing what Subsection (1)
giveth, Subsection (2) largely taketh away: the promise,
even if made, will be "binding" only within narrow limits.[183]
Furthermore, the use which is made in the Commentary of
two of our best known Good Samaritan cases contributes a
perhaps desirable confusion:

A gives emergency care to B's adult son while the son is
sick and without funds far from home. B subsequently prom-

ises to reimburse A for his expenses. The promise is not binding under this section.[184]

A saves B's life in an emergency and is totally and permanently disabled in so doing: One month later B promises to pay A $15 every two weeks for the rest of A's life, and B makes the payments for eight years until he dies. The promise is binding.[185]

The idea that § 89A [§ 86] has succeeded in "codifying" both the nineteenth century Massachusetts case and the twentieth century Alabama case is already sufficiently surprising but we are not yet finished:

A finds B's escaped bull and feeds and cares for it. B's subsequent promise to pay reasonable compensation to A is binding.[186]

Are we to believe that my promise to pay the stranger who takes care of my bull is binding but that my promise to pay the stranger who takes care of my dying son is not?[187] Or that "adult sons" are supposed to be able to take care of themselves while "escaped bulls" are not? Or that, as in maritime salvage law, saving property is to be rewarded but saving life is not?

Enough has been said to make the point that *Restatement (Second)*, at least in 89A [§ 86], is characterized by the same "schizophrenic quality" for which *Restatement (First)* was so notable.[188] This may well be all to the good. A wise draftsman, when he is dealing with novel issues in course of uncertain development, will deliberately retreat into ambiguity. The principal thing is that *Restatement (Second)* gives overt recognition to an important principle whose existence *Restatement (First)* ignored and, by implication denied. By the time we get to Restatement (Third) it may well be that § 89A [§ 86] will have flowered like Jack's bean-stalk in the same way that § 90 did between *Restatement (First)* and *Restatement (Second)*.

Classical theory used consideration as the touchstone for such curious deductions as that offers expressed to be irrevocable were nevertheless revocable until accepted, that certain modifications of ongoing contracts are ineffective and that discharges of debtors on payment of less than the full amount of the debt are not binding on creditors.[189] Each of these propositions, it should be noted, almost immediately generated an almost infinite number of exceptions to what was still proclaimed to be the "general rule." In the nature of things, it could not have been otherwise. Modifications may be agreed to or discharges granted honestly, fairly, voluntarily on both sides and in good faith; or they may be the result of coercion, economic duress, bad faith and fraud. In no civilized system of law will such extorted "agreements" be enforced; in our system, we explained that they were unenforceable because they lacked "consideration."[190] In any civilized system the same agreements, provided they are entered into voluntarily and in good faith, will be enforced —as of course they should be. We did that by discovering or inventing, in appropriate cases, "exceptions" from the "general rule"[191]—which makes the resulting pattern look a good deal more complicated than it really is, with the result that people—including lawyers and judges—are sometimes led astray. These extensions of consideration theory have also, since the 1930s, suffered considerable statutory erosion. The requirement of consideration for the irrevocability of offers, for modifications or for discharges was abolished in statutes enacted first in New York[192] and then copied in Michigan;[193] these statutory provisions were echoed in the Sales Article of the Uniform Commercial Code.[194] The effect of such statutory abolition of a consideration requirement will be, I suggest, to drive out into the open what has always been the underlying principle of decision—the distinction between good faith and bad faith agreements.[195]

The problem of the "illusory promise," which so greatly concerned many nineteenth century judges,[196] has been put to rest. The current approach is to say that if the promisor can be taken to have agreed to any limitation on his future freedom of action, however slight, then his promise is real and not illusory.[197] Indeed if an express promise is lacking, there is the prestigious authority of Cardozo to be cited to the proposition that courts are free to imply promises, to fill in missing terms and, in general, to pursue the beneficent end of making contracts for the parties.[198] And the once powerful slogan of "mutuality of obligation" makes its rare appearance nowadays as "the now exploded theory of mutuality of obligation."[199]

I suggested at an earlier point that the absolute liability idea was often preached but rarely practiced. I should indicate some of the techniques that were resorted to by way of avoidance. There is a series of American cases[200]—the

Massachusetts case from which I quoted the *Paradine v. Jane* language in the preceding lecture[201] was one of them — involving building or construction contracts in which the recurrent situation was that the structure, having been almost completed, was blown down or burnt down or sank into the mud—all without any fault being attributable to the builder. These were all pre-insurance cases—at least there is no indication in any of the cases that either the builder or the owner had insured his interest. In each of the cases owner sued builder. In each of the cases the court, giving judgment for plaintiff-owner, recited the *Paradine v. Jane* bit: the builder is not excused from the duty voluntarily assumed even by accident or inevitable necessity; if he wanted the excuse, he should have provided for it in his contract. The apparent meaning of the cases is that the unhappy builder must go on building, no matter how many times the structure collapses, all for the originally agreed contract price—or pay damages for not doing so. On closer examination, however, it turns out that all that was involved in the cases was the recovery of downpayments or progress payments made by the owner in course of construction—a result which might be described as a form of loss-sharing.[202] Toward the end of the century the courts succeeded in inventing an "exception" which, given the organization of the American construction industry, effectively neutralized the "general rule" of absolute liability. The "general rule," it was discovered, applied only to contracts in which the builder was to build the entire structure himself—it did not apply to contracts to repair or remodel existing structures (the exception came to be known as the "repair doctrine") or to contracts (or subcontracts) to build only part of a new structure.[203] With the advance of technology, the individual builder who built the whole house himself had disappeared; the heating contractor, the plumbing contractor, the electrical contractor and so on were all safely sheltered under the repair doctrine and were entitled to be paid for all they had done up to the moment of the catastrophe (the owner, the courts entertainingly explained, had, after all, received the "benefit" of their work[204]). Meanwhile it had, of course, become universal practice for owners to insure their interests —so everything worked out for the best in the best of all possible worlds.[205]

The law of sales is another area in which it is instructive to observe the working out of absolute liability theory in practice. It was early agreed that sellers were excused if, without fault, the goods contracted to be sold were damaged or destroyed before their risk had passed to the buyer.[206] This rule of excuse, originally developed in the context of contracts for the sale of specific goods, was in time extended to cover the cases of the farmer who had contracted to sell the crop to be grown on his land (but, because of a blight, there was no crop) and the manufacturer who had contracted to sell goods to be manufactured in his factory (but the factory burned down).[207] It was, the theoretical explanation ran, an "implied condition" of the contract that the goods, the crop or the factory should continue to be in existence. At this stage in the development, buyers were much more harshly treated than sellers. If, for example, the buyer's factory, warehouse, store, or residence was destroyed, so that he no longer had any use for the goods he had contracted to buy, that was no excuse for him—no "implied condition" was constructed in his favor and, as the courts liked to point out, "it is never impossible to pay money."[208] Relief for buyers—at least for professional buyers—came from one of the most curious of the late nineteenth century case law developments, which was proclaimed, on the highest level, almost simultaneously by the House of Lords in England and by the Supreme Court in the United States.[209] This development came to be known as the "perfect tender" rule.[210] In contracts between merchants, it was said, every aspect of the seller's performance was a true condition of the buyer' liability. If the seller deviated in the slightest degree from contract requirements—as to quality, quantity, time of delivery or method of shipment—the buyer was absolutely privileged to reject the goods, without regard to whether he had in any way been damaged or prejudiced by the deviation. Buyer's excuse under "perfect tender" was, of course, even broader than seller's excuse under the "implied condition" that the goods should continue to exist. "Perfect tender" continued to be gospel in sales law for a half century or more,[211] although it is undermined to a considerable degree in the Sales Article of the Uniform Commercial Code.[212]

There were, thus, many ways of avoiding the imposition of absolute liability in fact even while it was still being proclaimed in theory. But, even as the theoretical "general rule," the absolute liability idea began to break down a long time ago—although in this instance the breakdown seems to have begun earlier, and perhaps to have been carried further, in England than in this country. Traditionally, the problem of excuse by reason of change of circumstance had been discussed in terms of "impossibility." The literary vogue of *Paradine v. Jane* to the contrary notwithstanding, there came to be general agreement that "objective" (as distinguished from "subjective") impossibility of performance would operate as a discharge.[213] Shortly after the turn of the century the word "frustration" began to come in as a substitute for the word "impossibility."[214] As a term of art, "frustration" never acquired much precision or clarity of meaning; most of the time it was used as a sort of loose synonym for what had earlier been called "impossibility." And yet, from the beginning, there was a general understanding that the old theory of absolute—or almost absolute—liability was in process of dissolution. For one thing, putting the problem in terms of "frustration" made obsolete the idea that parties whose only contractual duty is to pay for what they receive are never discharged by change of circumstance because "it is never impossible to pay money." "Frustration" presupposed a two-way rule of discharge—applicable both to parties who pay and to parties who do—and indeed the Coronation cases, from which the "frustration" usage seems to have emerged, involved the discharge of paying parties, that is, people who had engaged rooms from which to view the procession that never took place.[215] But if parties who pay are to be discharged for something less than "objective impossibility," then, it would seem to follow, parties who do should equally be discharged for something less. And so they were. In time the liberalization of excuse under frustration theory reflected itself in a corresponding liberalization of excuse for mistake. "Mistake" and "frustration," it was pointed out, are merely two different ways of talking about the same thing[216]—that is, the real world has in some way failed to correspond with the imaginary world hypothesized by the parties to the contract. That there has been such a liberalization of excuse, under various theories, which has been going on for the past half century, is no longer seriously disputed by anyone, although there are stern moralists who feel that this is an unfortunate trend which should, if possible, be reversed.[217]

In this country, it remained fashionable for a considerable period to describe "frustration" as a doubtful English novelty[218]—a sensitive plant which would not flourish in our brisk transatlantic air. I do not think there is any reason to believe that the results in American courts were different from the results in English courts during that period, but I have not done the research that would be required to give my opinion any weight. The unresolved tensions in American attitudes toward "frustration" can be neatly illustrated in the treatment the problem receives in our two most notable twentieth century legal artifacts—the *First Restatement of Contracts* and the Uniform Commercial Code. The *Restatement* devoted a sternly moralistic chapter to the subject of Impossibility: only "objective impossibility" will prevent the formation of a contract or excuse its performance.[219] Two hundred sections earlier, in a completely different part of the *Restatement*, there was provided a broad and general rule of two-way discharge if "either party" finds his expectations "frustrated"—the English Coronation cases being, so to say, codified by way of a hypothetical case offered as an "illustration."[220] There were no cross-references in the *Restatement* between the Impossibility chapter and the Frustration section: you pay your money and you take your choice. The Sales Article of the Code contains a section which provides a broad rule of discharge for change of circumstance for sellers; nothing is said in the text of the section about a comparable discharge for buyers.[221] An official Comment to the section contributes this interesting thought: "[W]here the buyer's contract is in reasonable commercial understanding conditioned on a definite and specific venture or assumption . . . the reason of the present section may well apply and entitle the buyer to exemption." With such magnificently open-ended drafting we need not fear that the further development of the law will be in any way inhibited.

As theories of excuse have broadened, so, in a parallel development, have remedies for breach. In American commentary it has become a truism to say that the once exceptional remedy of specific performance is rapidly becoming the order of the day.[222] And the current edition of Williston collects an impressive number of cases in which courts have approved the award of punitive damages in "contract" actions without even bothering to go through the ritual of converting them into "tort" actions.[223] The old damage formulae, such as contract and market, have visibly lost their grip: as early as the mid-1950s it was possible for an astute commentator to conclude, citing an impressive number of cases decided mostly after 1940, that the recovery of lost profits in sales cases, in lieu of the contract and market differential, had become almost routine.[224] There are even indications that, with a lift from promissory estoppel theory and § 90 of the *Restatement,* consequential damages for breach of contracts to advance money are becoming available.[225]

Hadley v. Baxendale is still, and presumably always will be, a fixed star in the jurisprudential firmament. However, the nineteenth century gloss on *Hadley,* which Holmes popularized—the affirmative assumption of risk idea—has not been heard of these fifty years past.[226] I observed in our earlier discussion of *Hadley* that the damage formula which Baron Alderson stated is, taken by itself, affirmative and that the limitations of foreseeability and communication are easily manipulable. For the current meaning of the *Hadley* formula a House of Lords case, *The Heron II,* is instructive.[227] The action was by a charterer against a shipowner. The ship had been chartered to carry a cargo of sugar from Constanza to Basrah. In the course of the voyage the ship made what was found to have been an unjustifiable deviation, with the result that it arrived at Basrah nine days later than it otherwise would have. During the nine days the market price of sugar at Basrah had collapsed. The charterer sued the shipowner to recover damages for loss of market—that is the difference between what the sugar would have sold for if the ship had arrived on schedule and what the sugar actually sold for nine days later. The shipowner knew that the ship was carrying sugar for someone who intended to sell it in Basrah. The shipowner did not know whether the charterer intended to sell the sugar immediately on arrival or (this was considered to be an equally plausible alternative) to warehouse it for sale later in the year. Furthermore, the fact that the market price of sugar had collapsed during the nine-day delay was entirely accidental: the market price might equally well have remained stable or, for that matter, risen. On the facts so found, a unanimous House of Lords concluded that, under the rule of *Hadley v. Baxendale*, the charterer was entitled to his loss-of-market damages. As Lord Reid put it, the shipowner knew enough so that he should, as a reasonable shipowner, have realized that the loss which in fact was the consequence of the ship's delay was "not unlikely." And "not unlikely" was all that was required to cast the shipowner in damages under the twentieth century reading of the *Hadley* formula. In this country, we have not, as yet, had our *Heron II*; the case arising, there is no reason to believe that Anglo-American unity would be impaired.

We have now completed our survey of the brief, happy life of the general theory of contract, which had at most a hundred-year run. It is time to turn to what sort of answer we can give to the question we started with: Whatever happened to the theory of consideration? And, for that matter, where on earth did the theory of consideration come from in the first place?

IV

Conclusions
and Speculations

SPEAKING DESCRIPTIVELY, we might say that what
is happening is that "contract" is being reabsorbed into
the mainstream of "tort." Until the general theory of contract was hurriedly run up late in the nineteenth century,
tort had always been our residual category of civil liability.[228]
As the contract rules dissolve, it is becoming so again. It
should be pointed out that the theory of tort into which contract is being reabsorbed is itself a much more expansive
theory of liability than the theory of tort from which contract
was artificially separated a hundred years ago.[229]

We have had more than one occasion to notice the insistence of the classical theorists on the sharp differentiation
between contract and tort—the refusal to admit any liability in "contract" until the formal requisites of offer, acceptance and consideration had been satisfied, the dogma that
only "bargained-for" detriment or benefit could count as

consideration, and notably, the limitations on damage recovery.[230] Classical contract theory might well be described as an attempt to stake out an enclave within the general domain of tort. The dykes which were set up to protect the enclave have, it is clear enough, been crumbling at a progressively rapid rate. With the growth of the ideas of quasi-contract and unjust enrichment, classical consideration theory was breached on the benefit side. With the growth of the promissory estoppel idea, it was breached on the detriment side. We are fast approaching the point where, to prevent unjust enrichment, any benefit received by a defendant must be paid for unless it was clearly meant as a gift; where any detriment reasonably incurred by a plaintiff in reliance on a defendant's assurances must be recompensed.[231] When that point is reached, there is really no longer any viable distinction between liability in contract and liability in tort. We may take the fact that damages in contract have become indistinguishable from damages in tort as obscurely reflecting an instinctive, almost unconscious realization that the two fields, which had been artificially set apart, are gradually merging and becoming one.

A number of the developments which we noted in the preceding Lecture in tracing the twentieth century decline and fall from nineteenth century theory illustrate this basic coming together of contract and tort, as well as the "instinctive, almost unconscious" level on which the process has been working itself out.

The idea which we have come to know as "quasi-contract" was not part of the nineteenth century theory.[232] We think of quasi-contract as a sort of no-man's-land lying between contract and tort. In the early part of the century the concept served to blur the sharp edges both of contract theory and tort theory. It was, as the courts readily admitted, a legal fiction: the "quasi-contract" was no contract at all but the admitted legal fiction served, or so it was thought, the ends of justice.[233]

The "promissory estoppel" cases, like the quasi-contract cases, began to appear in the reports shortly after the turn of the century. The two concepts were, indeed, twins. As a matter of usage it came to be felt that quasi-contract was a better way of talking about the situation where plaintiff was seeking reimbursement for some benefit he had conferred on the defendant, while promissory estoppel was better for the situation where plaintiff was seeking recovery for loss or damage suffered as the result of reliance on the defendant's promises or representations. It would seem, as a matter of jurisprudential economy, that both situations could have been dealt with under either slogan but the legal mind has always preferred multiplication to division. And it may be that we still feel that the "benefit conferred" idea is a little closer to contract than it is to tort, so that contract (or quasi-contract) language is appropriate, while the "detrimental reliance" idea is a little closer to tort than it is to contract, so that tort (or quasi-tort) language is appropriate.

In this connection the introductory Comment to revised § 90 in *Restatement (Second)* is instructive:

> Obligations and remedies based on reliance are not peculiar to the law of contracts. This Section is often referred to in terms of "promissory estoppel," a phrase suggesting an

extension of the doctrine of estoppel. Estoppel prevents a person from showing the truth contrary to a representation of fact made by him after another has relied on the representation. . . . Reliance is also a significant feature of numerous rules in the law of negligence, deceit and restitution. . . . In some cases those rules and this Section overlap; in others they provide analogies useful in determining the extent to which enforcement is necessary to prevent injustice.[234]

We seem to be in the presence of the phenomenon which, in the history of comparative religion, is called syncretism—that is, according to Webster, "the reconciliation or union of conflicting beliefs." I have occasionally suggested to my students that a desirable reform in legal education would be to merge the first-year courses in Contracts and Torts into a single course which we could call Contorts. Perhaps the same suggestion would be a good one when the time comes for the third round of Restatements.

The most recent, and quite possibly the most important, development in the promissory estoppel or § 90 cases has been the suggestion that such contract-based defenses as the Statute of Frauds are not applicable when the estoppel (or reliance) doctrine is invoked as the ground for decision.[235] This line, if it continues to be followed, may ultimately provide the doctrinal justification for the fusing of contract and tort in a unified theory of civil obligation. A remarkable passage in the Restatement (Second) § 90 Commentary explains how most "contract" cases, if not all of them, can be brought under § 90 so that resort to § 75 [§ 71] and consideration theory will rarely, if ever, be necessary.[236] By passing through the magic gate of § 90, it seems, we can rid ourselves of all the technical limitations of contract theory. And if we choose to follow the alternative route of recovery under theories of quasi-contract or unjust enrichment—§ 89A [§ 86] in *Restatement (Second)*—the argument that the contract limitations no longer apply seems to be quite as strong as it is in the § 90 cases.[237] If we manage to get that far, the absurdity of attempting to preserve the nineteenth century contract-tort dichotomy will have become apparent even to the law professors who write law review articles and books—the academic mind is usually a generation or so behind the judicial mind in catching on to such things.

Until now the process of fusion has been going on mostly underground. I would like, however, to draw your attention to a sequence of recent California cases—during the past quarter of a century the California Supreme Court has unquestionably been the most innovative court in the country—which comes as close to an overt recognition of the process as anything I have yet seen in the judicial literature.

In *Lucas v. Hamm*[238] it appeared that an attorney had been directed by a testator to draft a will under which bequests were to go to certain beneficiaries. The attorney drafted the will in such a way that the bequests failed because of provisions which were invalid under the California rule against perpetuities. The Court declared, in an opinion which must have sent a thrill of horror through the California bar, that the attorney, if he had been negligent in drafting the will, would be liable to the beneficiaries in the amount of their loss. (Ultimately, the Court concluded that the attorney was not liable on the odd ground that the California rules on perpetuities were so confused that not even a competent attorney could be expected to understand them —hence there had been no negligence.) In its discussion of the attorney's theoretical liability the Court treated the case as a contract case involving the third party beneficiary doctrine. In *Connor v. Great Western Savings and Loan Association*,[239] the Savings and Loan Association had financed the builder of a residential development. The Association had, the Court found, "cooperated" closely with the builder and, indeed, "shared in the control" of the project. Under those circumstances, the Court held, in an opinion which must have horrified the banking community quite as much as *Lucas v. Hamm* had horrified the bar, that the Association was liable to the buyers of improperly built houses. The Court elected to treat the *Connor* case as an action in tort. *Heyer v. Flaig*[240] was, like *Lucas v. Hamm*, an action against an attorney by disappointed beneficiaries under a will. Strongly reaffirming the doctrine of *Lucas v. Hamm*, Tobriner, J., commented, in the course of his opinion in *Heyer v. Flaig*, that the discussion of contract theory in the *Lucas* case had been "conceptually superfluous since the crux of the action must lie in tort in any case; there can be no recovery without negligence." "It has been well established in this state," he continued, "that if the cause of action arises from a breach of a promise set forth in the contract, the action is ex contractu, but if it arises from a breach of duty growing out of the contract it is ex delicto." At least in the golden state of California, ex delicto seems to be well on the way toward swallowing up ex contractu.

100

One of the most interesting case law developments of recent years—one in which the California Court, once again, assumed a pioneering role[241]—has been the expansion of a manufacturer's liability to remote users of his defective products—the so-called "products liability" cases.[242] The law of seller's warranty, it is true, has always had one foot in contract and one foot in tort. Gradually, it seemed, the contract side of warranty had prevailed; the successive codifications in the Uniform Sales Act and the Sales Article of the Uniform Commercial Code had dealt with warranties entirely in contract terms. Beginning in the mid-1950s the courts, unexpectedly reversing the long established and apparently settled allocation of warranty liability to contract, set out to fashion a new and much more expensive law of warranty based entirely in tort. Here again, I suggest, we see an almost instinctive choice of tort over contract as the principle of liability in a rapidly developing field.

Restatement of Torts (Second) deals with products liability in § 402A, which has quickly become as celebrated as § 90 of the contracts Restatements:

> (1)   One who sells any product in a defective condition unreasonably dangerous to the user or consumer or to his property is subject to liability for physical harm thereby caused to the ultimate user or consumer, or to his property, if
>
> (a) the seller is engaged in the business of selling such product, and
>
> (b) it is expected to and does reach the user or

101

consumer without substantial change in the condition in which it is sold.

(2) The rule stated in Subsection (1) applies although

(a) the seller has exercised all possible care in the preparation and sale of his product, and

(b) the user or consumer has not bought the product from or entered into any contractual relation with the seller.[243]

The term "strict liability" has often been used to describe what has been going on in the cases as well as in § 402A. That is, no doubt, an exaggeration since liability is imposed on a "seller" only where his product is "defective" when sold and the defect makes it "unreasonably dangerous" to use. It has indeed been argued that the courts, by manipulating "defective" and "unreasonably dangerous," could quite as effectively restrict liability as ever they did in the hey-day of *caveat emptor*.[244] So they could, but it is entirely clear that, for the past ten or fifteen years, they have been manipulating the new catchwords in such a way as considerably to increase the liability of manufacturers and other commercial sellers to the users of their products. It should be noted that § 402A, by cutting the liability loose from its previously secure base in contract, at one stroke abolishes the "no privity of contract" defense, makes disclaimers of warranty ineffective and gets rid of the previously universal requirement of timely notice to the seller of the claimed "breach of warranty."

102

The products liability cases and the § 402A formulation impose liability even though the defendant has acted with "all possible care"—that is, even though he is in no way chargeable with negligence. It is not only on the products liability front that the erosion of the negligence idea has been proceeding.[245] Indeed the decline and fall of the nineteenth century idea that tort liability is, or should be, based on negligence or other fault matches the decline and fall of nineteenth century consideration and contract theory which we have been tracing in these Lectures. The two stories are, of course, halves of the same whole and the same "explosion of liability" has manifested itself, perhaps even more dramatically, on the tort side than on the contract side.

Let us assume, arguendo, that it is the fate of contract to be swallowed up by tort (or for both of them to be swallowed up in a generalized theory of civil obligation). We must still provide ourselves with an explanation of what contract—the classical or general theory of contract, as we have called it—was about in the first place and, if it is now dead or dying, what caused the fatal disease.

We started with Professor Friedman's suggestion that the "model" of classical contract theory bore a close resemblance to the "model" of what he calls "liberal"—or, I suppose, laissez-faire—economic theory.[246] In both models, as he put it, "parties could be treated as individual economic units which, in theory, enjoyed complete mobility and freedom of decision." I suppose that laissez-faire economic theory comes down to something like this: If we all do exactly as we please, no doubt everything will work out for the best. Which does seem to be about the same thing that

103

the contract theory comes down to, with liability reduced to a minimum and sanctions for breach cut back to the vanishing point. I do not mean to suggest—nor, I am sure, did Professor Friedman—that the lawyers and economists who constructed the two "models" were influenced by, or were even conversant with, each other's work. Holmes, for one, remained blissfully ignorant of economic theory throughout his life. It is rather that the lawyers and the economists, both responding to the same stimuli, produced theoretical systems which were harmonious with each other and which, in both cases, evidently responded to the felt needs of the time.

It seems apparent to the twentieth century mind, as perhaps it did not to the nineteenth century mind, that a system in which everybody is invited to do his own thing, at whatever cost to his neighbor, must work ultimately to the benefit of the rich and powerful, who are in a position to look after themselves and to act, so to say, as their own self-insurers. As we look back on the nineteenth century theories, we are struck most of all, I think, by the narrow scope of social duty which they implicitly assumed. No man is his brother's keeper; the race is to the swift; let the devil take the hindmost. For good or ill, we have changed all that. We are now all cogs in a machine, each dependent on the other. The decline and fall of the general theory of contract and, in most quarters, of laissez-faire economics may be taken as remote reflections of the transition from nineteenth century individualism to the welfare state and beyond.[247]

There are, I think, some other more specifically legal, factors which enter into the equation and which may help to explain why contract theory took on the particular shape it did as well as why it gradually lost its hold on the legal imagination.

Throughout the history of the Republic the achievement of at least a tolerable degree of national uniformity in the substantive law has been a pressing goal of law reform. Once the obvious solution of a federalization of the substantive law had been rejected on the constitutional level, the ominous prospect of a state-by-state fragmentation of the law became, as early as the 1820s, a matter of concern to thoughtful observers.[248] The prospect seemed particularly disturbing in the commercial law area where, as communications improved, transactions increasingly tended to spill over state lines. Codification, either partial or comprehensive, was early proposed as a solution[249] but the codification movement, after having enjoyed bright prospects for a generation or more, ran out of steam by the time of the Civil War if not before. Eventually the codification idea gained renewed strength and, after 1900, we witnessed a fairly comprehensive codification of commercial law in the series of Uniform Acts devoted to negotiable instruments, sales, documents of title and so on.[250] But from the 1860s until the 1900s the goal of national uniformity had to be pursued, as best it could, on the chancy level of case law.

A degree of federalization was, so to say, sneaked in the back door through the doctrine of the general federal commercial law announced by the Supreme Court of the United States, speaking through Justice Story, in *Swift v. Tyson*.[251] Over a considerable period of time this odd device worked extremely well: when the Supreme Court proposed a synthesis of conflicting views, the lower courts, state as well as federal, were, more often than not, delighted to go along.[252] The device, perhaps predictably, began to work less well as the political, economic and technological complexities and tensions of our society mounted and as the Supreme Court was forced to turn its energies in other directions. After 1900 the Supreme Court began to withdraw from the business of proposing new private law syntheses; with that balance-wheel no longer functioning, the whole *Swift v. Tyson* machine could no longer work and, as we know, eventually had to be scrapped.[253]

National uniformity on a case law level, in the federal republic we had evolved by mid nineteenth century, required what we might call an intensive purification of doctrine.[254] Almost instinctively, the so-called national law schools, led by the Harvard Law School under Langdell, seem to have set themselves to this task with, for fifty years or so, spectacular results. We should not underestimate the influence on the legal profession throughout the country of the handful of great law schools which, during this period, trained an inordinate number of the lawyers who became the leaders of bench and bar in every state. And, in addition to the immediate impact of teacher upon student in the classroom, there was the extraordinary series of monumental treatises which rolled forth in a steady flood. By the time of World War I the legal literature, which had previously consisted mostly of manuals written by practitioners for practitioners, had been revolutionized.

The basic idea of the Langdellian revolution seems to have been that there really is such a thing as the one true rule of law, universal and unchanging, always and everywhere the same—a sort of mystical absolute.[255] To all of us, I dare say, the idea seems absurd. We are steeped in the idea that law is process, flux, change; our relativism admits no absolutes. Had we lived a hundred years ago, I dare say that we too would have felt the compelling attraction of Langdell's simplistic jurisprudence. And, of course, so far as national uniformity in the law was concerned, Langdell's thesis ought to have been true even if it wasn't and perhaps, with a sufficient effort of will, beneficent error could be made to prevail over unpalatable truth.

For a riot of pure doctrine, nothing could have been better than Contract. Since there never had been a general theory of Contract before, there was nothing to inhibit the free play of the creative imagination—no historical underbush to be cleared away, no tangled skein of old doctrine to be set straight. Perhaps we must, after all, credit Langdell with a degree of genius for his perhaps instinctive choice of a nonexistent field as the vehicle for the initial demonstration of the great theory that law is doctrine and nothing but doctrine—pure, absolute, abstract, scientific—a logician's dream of heaven. And once the genius of Holmes had been enlisted in carrying the project out, the resulting theory could be guaranteed to be what the new age required.[256]

We have had occasion to note that one aspect of classical contract theory involved the avoidance of fact questions wherever possible as well as the restatement of questions of fact as questions of law through such devices as the reformulated doctrine of consideration and the newly minted objective theory of contract.[257] This insistence was of course consistent with the primarily doctrinal emphasis of the theory. I will also suggest that this aspect of the theory may be taken as reflecting an uneasy, inarticulate distrust of the role and function of the civil jury. To the extent that issues arising in contract litigation—in commercial litigation generally—can be phrased as questions of law for the court, the vagaries of juries can be effectively controlled. It is also true that appellate courts can exercise a much more thorough control over the vagaries of trial courts than would otherwise be the case—with a clear gain for the cause of pure doctrine. At the height of the classical period, it seemed that it was hardly possible to phrase any contract issue other than as a question of law. Everything came down to, or could be made to come down to, a question of consideration or of conditions or of the proper construction of a writing or of the applicable rule of damages—all these matters being for the court and not for the jury as well as coming within the proper scope of appellate review.

As an historian, I find the idea that distrust of the civil jury obscurely played some role in the causation of these events both intriguing and helpful. For one thing, on a broader level of historical reconstruction than the one I have attempted in these Lectures, we would be faced with the problem that the whole nineteenth century consideration episode was an Anglo-American exclusive which had no counterpart in the comparable industrial societies and legal systems of Western Europe. The peculiar Anglo-American institution of the civil jury, in the form which it assumed in the nineteenth century, might at least hint at an explanation of why what happened here did not happen in France and Germany and Scandinavia. For another thing, it seems to be true that the doctrinal statement of contract theory was carried to much greater extremes in this country than it ever was in England. For example, the English—compare any edition of Pollock on Contracts with Williston on Contracts—never went as far as we did with the bargain theory of consideration, wherefore it was unnecessary for English courts to experiment, as our courts did, with the promissory estoppel idea as an escape from bargain theory.[258] We may also observe that the English civil jury began its decline a good deal earlier than did the American version of the institution, which was riveted into the framework of the federal constitution. With us, too, the civil jury is on its way out; judges who propose that it be abolished need no longer fear impeachment proceedings. The disappearance of the civil jury may provide us with still another explanation for the collapse of classical contract theory. Since we no longer have to worry much about juries, we need no longer be as reluctant as once we were to allow trial courts—as triers of the facts—to inquire into such essentially factual questions as good faith, reasonableness, observance of commercial standards, change of circumstance, or, for that matter, fraud, duress and coercion.

It may be that, in totally unexpected ways, things work out for the best. In the First Restatement the debate between Williston and Corbin (or their principals, Holmes and Cardozo) resulted in an uneasy and, it might be argued, intellectually indefensible stand-off. We can see by hindsight that Corbin and Cardozo had a better understanding than did their opponents of the course on which the law was set. If truth means the ability to predict what is going to happen

109

next, they were closer to the truth. And yet, if their approach had prevailed—if consideration had been defined as the equivalent of causa[259]—it is entirely possible that the collapse of the classical theory might have been delayed for another generation or so and might have come about in an altogether different fashion. The Cardozo-Corbin construct did retain a central feature of the old theory—that conclusions are to be expressed as deductions from rules of law, not as deductions from observed facts. Their approach would have introduced a good deal more play into the joints of contract theory and, thereby, perhaps, have allowed it to survive, in recognizable form, for a considerable time. One way of staving off a revolution is to make concessions to the revolutionary demands even before the demands have been precisely formulated. The Restatement compromise was to maintain the structure of classical theory in all its formal rigidity, while ambiguously hinting—as in § 90—that there might be possible routes of escape. Had the structure itself been, so to say, modernized or made more habitable, the courts, in making good their escape, might not have been compelled to tear the whole thing down. The unresolved tensions of the First Restatement, which admirably reflected the intellectual cross-currents of the post–World War I period, may thus have largely contributed, in ways that the draftsmen never intended and could not possibly have foreseen, to the emergence of what we begin to perceive as a radically new way of analyzing the problem of civil obligation.

This has been a study in what might be called the process of doctrinal disintegration. The process is one with which we have been, until now, relatively unfamiliar. The reduction of the basic fields of law to self-contained and logically consistent systems of rule and doctrine was, I suggest, the principal feature, as it was the greatest achievement, of our late nineteenth century and early twentieth century jurisprudence. What went on in Contract is merely a special instance of what went on everywhere. The instinctive hope of the great system-builders was, no doubt, that the future development of the law could be, if not controlled, at least channeled in an orderly and rational fashion. That hope has proved, in our century of war and revolution, delusive. The systems have come unstuck and we see, presently, no way of glueing them back together again. But it is possible to learn as much from a failed experiment as from a successful one. Our observation of how the general theory of contract was put together and how it fell apart may stand us in good stead when next we feel ourselves in a mood to build something.

I have one final thought. We have become used to the idea that, in literature and the arts, there are alternating rhythms of classicism and romanticism. During classical periods, which are, typically, of brief duration, everything is neat, tidy and logical; theorists and critics reign supreme; formal rules of structure and composition are stated to the general acclaim. During classical periods, which are, among other things, extremely dull, it seems that nothing interesting is ever going to happen again. But the classical aesthetic, once it has been formulated, regularly breaks down in a protracted romantic agony. The romantics spurn the exquisitely stated rules of the preceding period; they experiment, they improvise; they deny the existence of any rules; they churn around in an ecstasy of self-expression. At the height of a romantic period, everything is confused, sprawling, formless and chaotic—as well as, frequently, extremely interesting. Then, the romantic energy having spent itself, there is a new classical reformulation—and so the rhythms continue.

Perhaps we should admit the possibility of such alternating rhythms in the process of the law. We have witnessed the dismantling of the formal system of the classical theorists. We have gone through our romantic agony—an experience peculiarly unsettling to people intellectually trained and conditioned as lawyers are. It may be that, in this centennial year, some new Langdell is already waiting in the wings to summon us back to the paths of righteousness, discipline, order, and well-articulated theory. Contract is dead—but who knows what unlikely resurrection the Easter-tide may bring?

NOTES

As noted in the foreword, bracketed references to the *Restatement of Law (Second) Contracts* (1981) have been added, where necessary, by the editor.

Introduction

1. One of the most comprehensive statements of the approach which I am tendentiously and no doubt unfairly characterizing is to be found in a *Symposium on The Relevance of Contract Theory*, 1967 Wisc. L. Rev. 303 *et seq.* The Wisconsin *Symposium* consists of an introductory note by Professor Malcolm Sharp plus the following papers which were originally read at a panel discussion at the 1966 annual meeting of the Association of American Law Schools: Friedman and Macaulay, "Contract Law and Contract Teaching: Past, Present, and Future"; Speidel, "Contract Law: Some Reflections upon Commercial Context and the Judicial Process"; Mueller, "Business Fact and Legal Fantasy."

Professor Stewart Macaulay, co-author of the lead article in the *Symposium*, is no doubt entitled to rank as Lord High Executioner of the Contract is Dead school. During the past ten years or so Professor Macaulay had published a series of highly interesting articles on the irrelevance of traditional contract theory. See, e.g., his *Non-Contractual Relations in Business: A Preliminary Study*, 28 Am. Sociological Rev. 55 (1963).

113

Professor Lawrence Friedman, co-author with Professor Macaulay of the *Symposium* article, has written, in his *Contract Law in America* (1965), one of the most original and thoughtful analyses of the development of contract theory which has yet appeared. For an extended quotation from Professor Friedman's book, see text at note 6 *infra*.

I. Origins

2. The reference is to Dean Langdell's casebook on Contracts (1871) which is discussed in the text following note 19 *infra*.

3. On the "absurd miscalculations," see Morison, Admiral of the Ocean Sea, a Life of Christopher Columbus (1942).

4. The first edition of *Williston on Contracts* appeared in 1920. A second edition appeared in 1936. A third edition by Professor Walter Jaeger has been in course of publication since 1957.

5. The first edition of *Corbin on Contracts* appeared in 1950. Professor Corbin continued to work on revisions until sometime in the 1960s when his failing health made it impossible for him to continue. Several of the original volumes were completely done over and were reissued with later publication dates.

6. Friedman, Contract Law in America 20–24 (1965).

7. I assume that Professor Friedman's "liberal nineteenth century economics" refers to what is often described as laissez-faire. See text following note 246 *infra* where this idea is further discussed. The close relationship between nineteenth century contract theory and "the philosophy of laissez-faire" is also suggested in Atiyah, An Introduction to the Law of Contract at 3 (2d ed. 1971). The author, who received his training in England, is Professor of Law at the Australian National University. It is not without interest that the same novel insight should have suggested itself, to both English-trained and American-trained theorists who, presumably, arrived at their conclusions independently of each other.

Professor Atiyah also assumes, as both Professor Friedman and I do, that Anglo-American contract theory is a relatively recent creation. He comments: "Although much of the English law of contract has roots going back to the Middle Ages, most of the general principles were developed and elaborated in the eighteenth and nineteenth centuries." (*Id.* at 2.) Farnsworth, *Legal Remedies for Breach of Contract*, 70 Colum. L. Rev. 1145, 1216 (1970) also stresses the relationship between contract theory and "the economic philosophy of free enterprise"; see the quotation from Professor Farnsworth's article in note 125 *infra*.

8. Perhaps "grow" or "develop" would be closer to the mark than "change." A theory which is incapable of growth or development can of course die—which is indeed what happened.

9. Friedman, *op. cit. supra* note 6, at 24.

10. I assume that this is what Professor Atiyah had in mind in his comment, quoted in note 7 *supra*, that English contract law has "roots" which go back to the Middle Ages but no "general principles" which antedate the eighteenth century.

11. The Report appears in J. Story, Miscellaneous Writings at 698 (W. W. Story ed. 1852). The attribution of the Report to Story was made by his son, William Wetmore Story, who edited his father's papers, and appears to be unquestionable.

12. *Id.* at 712.

13. *Id.* at 730–31. In the passage of the Report immediately preceding the language quoted, Story did refer to "a law of contracts" but in such a way as to make it clear that in his thought there were many kinds of contracts rather than a single theory of contract. See the language quoted in note 16 *infra* from the "Advertisement" to the second edition of William Wetmore Story's *Treatise on the Law of Contract.*

14. According to the notice on William Wetmore Story in *28*

Dictionary of American Biography (1936), 109, his interest in sculpture was first aroused when the trustees of the Mount Auburn Cemetery in Cambridge commissioned him to do a statue of his late father. On the merits of his life's work, which also included several volumes of poetry, the *D.A.B.* comments: "Without being in any direction a genius, Story learned the secret of happiness by the wise development of his many talents." After his death in 1895 Henry James, a long-time friend, wrote a two volume biography, *William Wetmore Story and His Friends* (1903).

15. On Story, see the admirable biographical study by Dunne, Justice Joseph Story and the Rise of the Supreme Court (1970).

16. William Wetmore Story did indeed bring out a *Treatise on the Law of Contracts not under Seal* (1844) which he revised and expanded in a second edition (1847). How far we still are from anything like a general theory of contract is sufficiently indicated by the following quotation from the "Advertisement" to the Second Edition (p. v): "Many new branches of the subject of Contracts have been introduced, which were not treated of in the former edition, among which may be mentioned the law relating to Usury, and to the contracts of Factors, Brokers, Auctioneers, Executors and Administrators, Trustees, Seamen, Corporations, Guardian and Ward, and Masters of Ships." There are chapters on Bailments, Sale of Personal Property, Guaranty and Landlord and Tenant. Two relatively brief chapters on Mutual Assent and The Consideration are about the sum of the theoretical discussion.

Parsons on Contracts (1853) also turns out to be, on examination, simply a treatment, seriatim, of the several types of "commercial contracts" identified by Justice Story and analyzed in his own Commentaries and in his son's two Treatises. Theophilus Parsons was the Dane Professor of Law at the Harvard Law School from 1848 until 1870 when, shortly before Langdell's appointment as dean, he retired. See Sutherland, The Law at Harvard 150 *et seq.* (1967).

17. I have myself contributed to the spread of what now seems to me to be a misreading of history: "The assumed unity of contract law has always marked a centrifugal tendency. The law of sales, the law of insurance, the law of labor agreements, to take three examples, all have (or once had) their roots in contract; sales law and insurance law have long since become, and labor law is clearly in process of becoming, independent of the general law of contract." (Kessler and Gilmore, Contracts: Cases and Materials 117 [1970].) I should have written that sales law and insurance law were established as specialties before Contract had ever been heard of. On the twentieth century relationship between labor law and Contract, see Summers, *Collective Agreements and the Law of Contracts*, 78 Yale L.J. 552 (1969). Professor Lawrence Friedman apparently shares, at least to some extent, the idea that Contract came first and then the specialties split off. See the quotation from his Contract Law in America, text at note 6 *supra*. The misconception, if it is one, has deep roots. Thus Williston in the Preface to the first edition of his treatise on Contracts wrote: "[T]he law on contracts suffers from a difficulty opposite to that which has hampered the development of the law of torts. That law grew up piecemeal and with limitations varying in different forms of action. Only in recent years has much effort been made to knit together with broad fundamental principles the various kinds of torts. The law of contracts, on the other hand after starting with some degree of unity now tends from its very size to fall apart." (1 Williston, Contracts xi [3d ed. Jaeger 1957].) Williston gives insurance law and suretyship law as illustration of the tendency of contract law to "fall apart."

18. As to the "premature old age" of negotiable instruments law: the "holder in due course" concept was worked out by Lord Mansfield and his successors in the late eighteenth and early nineteenth centuries against a business background in which bills of exchange and promissory notes did in fact circulate and could be

expected to pass through a number of hands before being retired. As the modern banking system developed, instruments gradually ceased to circulate. In this century nothing is rarer than a true negotiation to a third party purchaser for value—the use of negotiable notes which pass from dealer to finance company in the attempt to carry out consumer frauds is hardly a "true negotiation." The whole "holder in due course" concept could usefully have been abolished when negotiable instruments law was codified at the end of the nineteenth century. In fact it was preserved like a fly in amber both in the N.I.L. and in its successor, Article 3 of the Uniform Commercial Code. Indeed our codifications typically preserve once vital but now obsolete concepts in much the same way that our museums preserve the ancient artifacts of bygone civilizations. I have commented on this aspect of the problem of codification in a paper, *On Statutory Obsolescence*, 39 Colo. L. Rev. 461 (1967). On the functional obsolescence of the "holder in due course" concept, see Rosenthal, *Negotiability— Who Needs It?* 71 Colum. L. Rev. 375 (1971).

19. By way of illustration of the "back-lash effect," consider the late nineteenth century sales rule of "perfect tender," discussed in the text at note 210 *infra*.

20. Sutherland, The Law at Harvard (1967) devotes chapter 6 to the Langdell Era: 1870–1895. Born in New Hampshire in 1826 Langdell studied law at Harvard from 1851 to 1854, supporting himself by serving as the Law School's librarian. Thereafter he practiced law in New York for sixteen years. He returned to Harvard, at President Eliot's invitation, in 1870, served as Dean from 1870 until 1895, retired from the faculty in 1900 and died in 1906. Apart from the casebook on Contracts (plus the Summary) and a second casebook on Sales (1872), he seems to have written little or nothing. Such student comments as have survived suggest that he was a less than inspiring teacher—although it is of course possible that the student reaction, at least in the early years, was

colored by hostility to his novel method of teaching from the cases instead of lecturing.

Professor Sutherland notes that Langdell, as a student, had worked as a sort of research assistant for Parsons, who was then preparing his treatise on Contracts (see note 16 *supra*). Conceivably his work with Parsons may have had something to do with his choice of Contracts as the subject for the first casebook. Or it may simply be that, after Parson's retirement, Langdell had inherited the Contracts course and put the casebook together because that was the course he was scheduled to teach.

Professor Sutherland reproduces an astonishing portrait of Langdell ("painted . . . in the twenty-second year of [His] deanship") which could perfectly well be a portrait of the original Christopher Columbus.

21. Sutherland, The Law at Harvard 159 (1967).

22. Langdell enlarged on what he meant by "Law . . . as a science" in a speech which he gave to the Harvard Law School Association in 1886. Commenting on the situation which he found when he became Dean in 1870, he said: "[It] was indispensable to establish at least two things; first that law is a science; secondly, that all the available materials of that science are contained in printed books. . . . [T]he library is the proper workshop of professors and students alike; . . . it is to us all that the laboratories of the university are to the chemists and physicists, all that the museum of natural history is to the geologists, all that the botanical garden is to the botanists." (Sutherland, The Law at Harvard 175 [1967]. Professor Sutherland also reprints [at 174] the passage from the preface to the casebook quoted in the text.)

23. See text at note 6 *supra*.

24. See text at note 13 *supra* and note 16 *supra*.

25. This paragraph and the two paragraphs which follow will

be allowed to remain in an almost pure state of abstraction with little or no attempt at documentation. To the extent that documentation can be provided at this level of generalization, authorities will be cited as the discussion proceeds.

26. Holmes, The Common Law 236 ([1881] Howe ed. 1963).

27. As to Lord Coke's views, see Bromage v. Genning, 1 Rolle 368 (K.B. 1616): Specific performance of a convenant to make a lease "would subvert the intention of the convenantor when he intends it to be at his election either to lose the damages or to make the lease, and they wish to compel him to make the lease against his will. . . ." For Holmes's approval of *Bromage v. Genning*, see his address, *The Path of the Law* (1897), in his Collected Legal Papers 175, (1920), restating a position he had earlier taken in The Common Law, *supra* note 26 at 235–36.

28. *Op. cit. supra* note 26, at 236.

29. For this and the preceding citations, see the lecture on *Trespass and Negligence*, in The Common Law 67 ([1881] Howe ed. 1963).

30. *Id.* at 76, 77.

31. Posner, *A Theory of Negligence*, 1 Journal of Legal Studies 28 (1972) restates and defends Holmes's theories of tort liability.

32. Thus in Hawkes, v. Saunder, 1 Cowper 289, 98 Eng. Rep. 1091 (K.B. 1782) (holding the promise of an executrix to pay a legacy "in consideration of assets" enforceable) Mansfield is reported to have said: "Where a man is under a moral obligation, which no Court of Law or Equity can inforce, and promises, the honesty and rectitude of the thing is a consideration . . . [T]he ties of conscience upon an upright mind are a sufficient consideration." And in Pillans and Rose v. Van Mierop and Hopkins, 3 Burr. 1663, 97 Eng. Rep. 1035 (K.B. 1765) he had denied the need for any sort of consideration in what we might call a commercial context:

"I take it, that the ancient notion about the want of consideration was for the sake of evidence only; for when it is reduced to writing, as in convenants, specialties, bonds, etc., there was no objection to the want of consideration. . . . In commercial cases among merchants, the want of consideration is not an objection." On the affinity between Mansfield's views and the idea of *causa* as it has come down into the civil law systems from Roman law, see 8 Holdsworth, A History of English Law 42 *et seq.* (2nd ed. 1937).

33. See 8 Holdsworth, *op. cit. supra* note 32, at 34 *et seq.* Eastwood v. Kenyon, 11 Ad. & E. 438, 113 Eng. Rep. 482 (Q.B. 1840) is usually taken as symbolizing the definitive rejection of Mansfield's ideas.

34. Thus, 2 Kent, Commentaries on American Law 465 (4th ed. 1840): "A valuable consideration is one that is either a benefit to the party promising, or some trouble or prejudice to the party to whom the promise is made. Any damage, or suspension, or forbearance of a right will be sufficient to sustain a promise." The fourth edition, from which the passage is quoted, was copyrighted by Chancellor Kent and was presumably prepared by him. Holmes, who edited the twelfth edition of *Commentaries* (1872), let the passage stand without comment.

Story, A Treatise on the Law of Contracts Not under Seal § 431 (2d ed. 1847): "The principal requisite, and that which is the essence of every consideration, is, that it should create some benefit to the party promising, or some trouble, prejudice, or inconvenience to the party to whom the promise is made; wherever, therefore, any injury to the one party, or any benefit to the other party springs from a consideration, it is sufficient to support a contract."

Parsons on Contracts 444 (1853) is to the same effect as Kent and Story.

The list could be indefinitely extended, with quotations from treatises and judicial opinions both English and American. Thus Parker, J., in Hamer v. Sidway, 124 N.Y. 538, 543, 27 N.E. 413 (1891) quotes from an English case (Currie v. Misa, L.R. 10 Ex. 152,

162 [1875]): "A valuable consideration in the sense of the law may consist either in some right, interest, profit or benefit accruing to the one party, or some forbearance, detriment, loss or responsibility given, suffered or undertaken by the other." *Hamer v. Sidway* itself illustrates a point which will be subsequently discussed (see text at and following note 136 *infra*), which is that the New York Court of Appeals (unlike most American courts) consistently rejected the so-called bargain theory of consideration formulated by Holmes. In *Hamer v. Sidway* it was held (on a curious amalgam of contract and trust theory) that an uncle's promise to pay his nephew $5000 if the nephew refrained, until his twenty-first birthday, from drinking, smoking, swearing, and playing cards or billiards for money was (the nephew having so refrained) enforceable against the uncle's estate.

35. The Common Law 227–30 ([1881] Howe ed. 1963).

36. In volume 2 of his projected biography of Holmes, *The Proving Years 1870–1882* (1963), the late Mark DeWolfe Howe commented (p. 245), with respect to "the thesis which inspired the three lectures on contract," that "one must recognize that he was urging a revolutionary change in legal thought." Professor Howe's analysis of the "revolutionary" nature of Holmes's contract theories emphasizes the Holmesian "paradox" that there is no moral duty to perform a contractual obligation (see text at note 28 *supra;* Howe, *op. cit.* at 233 *et seq.*) and Holmes's insistence on an "objective" as opposed to a "subjective" approach to the problem of contractual liability (see text at the beginning of the following Lecture; Howe, *op. cit.* at 243 *et seq.*). The epithet, as I have been attempting to show, seems no less apt when applied to the bargain theory of consideration. On the non-historical or a-historical nature of *The Common Law*, see Professor Howe's sensitive and perceptive introduction to his 1963 edition: "*The Common Law* is not primarily a work of legal history. It is an endeavor in philosophy —a speculative undertaking in which the author sought to find in

the materials of legal history data which would support a new interpretation of the legal order." (P. xx.) Holmes, like any revolutionary, merely sought to sugar over his more startling heresies with a frosting of antique learning.

37. On Holmes's prodigious scholarly labors during the 1870s, see generally Howe, *op. cit. supra* note 36.

38. He discusses at some length (in passages which I have omitted in the quotation at note 34 *supra*) the celebrated case of Coggs v. Bernard, 2 Ld. Raym. 909, 92 Eng. Rep. 107 (K.B. 1702), holding that one who undertakes to carry goods safely is responsible for any damage to the goods even though he was not a common carrier and was to have nothing for his work. Most of the cases which Holmes cites in his discussion of consideration come in the course of his *Coggs v. Bernard* discussion, the point of which was that, despite the "popular belief" that liability in the case was based on consideration theory, the "true explanation" (which Holmes had given in an earlier lecture on Bailments) was that the case had nothing to do with consideration or contract but was simply an illustration of the old tort idea of liability for misfeasance (as distinguished from nonfeasance). There is a disapproving reference to two English cases as illustrations of the tendency of the courts to "obliterate" the distinction between bargained-for consideration and mere "detriment." In support of his own formulation he contents himself with a reference to Ellis v. Clarke, 110 Mass. 389 (1872) (holding, according to Holmes, that there would be no consideration for the defendant's endorsement of a promissory note if the defendant had not known that the holder of the note intended to alter his position in reliance on the endorsement) and to the class of cases which hold that a reward cannot be claimed by a person who has performed the required services without knowing of the existence of the offer to pay the reward (citing Fitch v. Snedaker, 38 N.S. 248 [1868]). Perhaps Holmes would have been better advised if he had omitted any attempt to show that his

theory had any support in the case law, English or American.

39. On contemporary reactions to *The Common Law*, see Howe, *op. cit. supra* note 36, at 246 *et seq.* I am happy to find myself in agreement with Professor Howe on the effect which Holmes had on Williston: "One may be thoroughly confident that it was through his reading of Holmes—both as jurist and as judge—that Samuel Williston, the father of contemporary doctrine with respect to contract in Anglo-American law, was led to an acceptance of the fundamentals of Holmes's doctrine." (*Id.* at 246–47.) It is of course an exaggeration to suggest that there was no dissent from the new dispensation. Dean Ames of the Harvard Law School was one notable figure of the time who had his reservations, see his *Two Theories of Consideration,* 12 Harv. L. Rev., 515 (1899). For an interchange between Ames and Holmes with respect to an earlier article in which Ames had questioned some of Holmes's history, see Howe, *op. cit. supra* note 36, at 230.

40. That consideration is defined in Holmesian terms in both Restatements is not the end of the story for either Restatement. The first or original *Restatement of the Law of Contracts* (1932) will be discussed in the text *infra* following note 134. The *Restatement of the Law (Second) Contracts* (Tentative Draft No. 2, 1965) will be discussed in the text *infra*, following note 163.

41. This comment was a handwritten annotation in Holmes's own copy of *The Common Law* which is reproduced in the Howe edition (1963) at 230. The annotation referred to the statement in the lecture on Elements of Contract that: "It is said that consideration must not be confounded with motive. It is true that it must not be confounded with what may be the prevailing or chief motive in actual fact." (For the context in which the statement appears, see the extended quotation, text at note 35 *supra.*)

42. There is not a single reference in any of the lectures to the possibility of quasi-contractual relief. Nor is there any suggestion that liability in tort might provide an escape route from the theory of contract as Holmes formulated it.

43. Holmes did not, in the contract lectures in *The Common Law*, address himself to these subsidiary propositions. They were worked out, principally by Williston, in the following generation; the best place in which to observe them is in the first edition of *Williston on Contracts* (1920). Williston, in his extrapolations, was unquestionably faithful to the spirit of the master's thought. As the hazards of litigation brought such questions before Holmes as judge, his responses were consistent with the Willistonian gloss. For an example, see note 71 *infra*.

44. 2 Ch. D. 463 (C.A. 1876).

45. There are two reports of Stilk v. Myrick: 6 Esp. 129, 170 Eng. Rep. 851; 2 Camp. 317, 170 Eng. Rep. 1168 (1809). For a curious discrepancy between the two reports, see text following note 53 *infra*.

46. 9 App. Cas. 605 (H.L. 1884).

47. 1 Williston, Contracts § 130 (1920). The passage quoted continues to appear without change (although a couple of additional statements have been interpolated) in the current (third) edition of *Williston* by Professor Jaeger.

48. Williston's citations were notoriously inaccurate. The correct citation for Harris v. Watson is Peake, 102 (170 Eng. Rep. 94). The case was decided in 1791.

49. This is the form in which the supporting footnote appeared in the original (1920) edition. In the current edition by Professor Jaeger the text is unchanged except as stated in note 47 *supra* but the sequence of footnotes has been changed. The

principal case cited to the text in the current edition is an American case, Lingenfelder v. Wainwright Brewing Co., 103 Mo. 578, 15 S.W. 844 (1890). The two English cases now appear at the end of a string citation in a note which is appended to the statement in the text: "Numerous other cases support this principle." Evidently Williston is in the process of being Americanized. The use which Williston, Langdell *et al.* made of the English cases in putting the general theory of contract together will be discussed hereafter, see text at and following note 126 *infra*.

50. Lord Kenyon's reference at this point was to another aspect of the maritime law rule under which, if the ship (and consequently the freight) was lost, the surviving seamen lost their claim for wages. Only if the freight was earned did the wages become payable. It later became customary to provide in bills of lading that the freight was to be regarded as earned "vessel lost or not lost."

51. 170 Eng. Rep. 94.

52. Both reports of the case, see note 45 *supra*, are in agreement on the way in which counsel attempted to distinguish *Harris v. Watson* from the case at bar. I quote from the report in Espinasse, 170 Eng. Rep. 851.

53. See note 45 *supra*.

54. See note 45 *supra*.

55. An odd detail of the case is that Espinasse, with the Attorney General, appeared as counsel for the plaintiff seamen. One might suppose that he would get one of his own cases right. On the other hand he may have been so distracted by his duties as counsel that he was unable to jot down as a full report of Lord Ellenborough's remarks (which were, of course, delivered orally) as Campbell, who was not involved except as reporter.

56. See note 32 and note 33 *supra* and the accompanying text.

57. See text at note 52 *supra*. Perhaps a third explanation, albeit a scurrilous one, of what Lord Ellenborough was about is suggested by a note to the Campbell report of *Stilk v. Myrick* (170 Eng. Rep. 1169). The note refers to an anonymous case which Lord Ellenborough had decided in 1806 in which he had held that a seaman who had been taken from on board a merchant ship and forcibly impressed into the Royal Navy had no claim for wages for the time he had served on the merchant ship before his impressment. This holding was in the teeth of a statute which provided, as clearly as language can, that an impressed seaman did not forfeit his claim for pre-impressment wages on a merchant ship. The tone of the note suggests that the holding was considered scandalous. So the uninteresting truth may conceivably be that Lord Ellenborough was an owner's man all the way who would use any theory, however far-fetched—even "want of consideration"—to strike down seamen's wage claims.

58. For Williston's statement of the "rule," see the quotation in the text at note 47 *supra*.

59. Bartlett v. Wyman, 14 Johns. 260 (Sup. Ct. N.Y. 1817) deserves mention. This was another case in which seamen sought to enforce a promise by the master to pay them extra wages for going forward with the voyage. The circumstances of the New York case were that a rumor that a congressional embargo was about to be placed on shipping (during the Napoleonic wars) had led to a rise in seamen's wages. (It seems odd that the rumor should have had this effect but this is what we are told [14 Johns. at 26]. Perhaps the increased wages reflected the dangers that would be encountered if the ships sailed in violation of the embargo.) In the *Bartlett* case the crew of a vessel, which was lying in port at Savannah, who had signed on at the lower wages, had threatened to jump ship unless they were paid more. The seamen lost their case in New York as

they had done in England. *Bartlett v. Wyman* shows up, without special mention, in the string citation which Williston gives to support his statement of the rule, text at note 47 *supra*, and it is true that in Schwartzreich v. Bauman-Basch, Inc., 231 N.Y. 196, 131 N.E. 887 (1921) the Court of Appeals referred to *Bartlett* as having been decided on consideration theory. The *Bartlett* opinion itself suggests that the court was more concerned with the possibility of economic coercion than it was with consideration theory. Almost simultaneously with *Bartlett v. Wyman* the New York Supreme Court decided Lattimore v. Harsen, 14 Johns. 330 (Sup. Ct. N.Y. 1817) in which it held that there was no objection on grounds of consideration theory to a modification agreement under which the City of New York agreed to pay a contractor considerably more than the original price for opening a "cartway" on 70th Street. *Lattimore v. Harsen* appears in a string citation in the footnote in which Williston collects cases which represent a "contrary viewpoint" (from the true doctrine) which had prevailed "in a few jurisdictions" (see the text following note 49 *supra*). Williston was apparently not in the least concerned that he had New York cases on both sides of the equation. On the New York case law, and twentieth century statutory developments, see the interesting Comment, *Modification of a Contract in New York: Criteria for Enforcement*, 35 U. of Chi. L. Rev. 173 (1967).

60. 2 Ch. D. 463 (C.A. 1876).

61. Mellish, L. J., and James, L. J., delivered opinions. A third judge, Baggallay, J. A., merely noted that he "entirely" concurred in the "judgements which have been pronounced." Mellish and James were in agreement not only on how the case should be decided but also on why it should be decided that way. The Mellish opinion, for no particular reason, seems to be better known; at least it is more frequently reprinted in the Contracts casebooks than the James opinion.

62. For more on Mellish and "meeting of the minds" theory, see the discussion of *Raffles v. Wichelhaus*, text following note 85 *infra*.

63. "Obviously" is a word which lawyers tend to use when they are dealing with exceptionally obscure matters. The correct decision in *Dickinson v. Dodds* had not been obvious to the vice-chancellor before whom the case had been tried. Bacon, V.C., had indeed decreed before specific performance in favor of Dickinson, for which he was reversed on appeal. The Vice-Chancellor was not necessarily in theoretical disagreement with his superiors; he seems to have been concerned by an odd circumstance in the facts of the case, which was that Dodds had not communicated his revocation directly to Dickinson, who had learned of the sale to Allen (taken as tantamount to a revocation) indirectly from someone named Berry. To Mellish and his colleagues it made no difference whatever that Dodds had not even attempted to let Dickinson know that he was withdrawing the offer. (Berry's intervention seems to have been purely fortuitous: he was apparently merely a busybody and was not in any sense an agent or emissary for Dodds.) Indeed Mellish's opinion wobbles and waffles back and forth on whether any knowledge, direct or indirect, of the revocation on Dickinson's part was necessary. At one point Mellish analogizes the *Dickinson v. Dodds* situation to the case of an offeror who dies before his offer has been accepted where it is "admitted law" that the death terminates the offeree's power to accept. "Meeting of the minds" theory, carried to the extreme limit of its logic, would make knowledge of the revocation by the offeree irrelevant: if the minds didn't meet, they didn't meet (although evidence that the offeror had in fact changed his mind could have been required). Since Dickinson had learned of Dodd's change of mind from Berry, it was not necessary to carry the theory to such an extreme but there are indications that at least Mellish might have been willing to go all the way.

64. I shall take up the switch from the "subjective" to the "objective" approach and its relevance to the general theory of contract at the beginning of the next Lecture.

65. For the conventional explanation of the "rule," see 1 Williston, Contracts § 55 *et seq.* (3rd ed. by Jaeger). In substance the text follows that of the original (1920) edition although the footnotes have once again been "Americanized" (see n. 49 *supra*). Williston assumes that the revocation is "not effectual until communicated" (§ 56) but adds (§ 57) that the "communication" may, as in *Dickinson v. Dodds*, be "indirect." He comments that this aspect of the rule has been "severely criticized in the United States" but indicates his own approval.

66. That is, a consideration for the assurance of irrevocability, separate from, or independent of, the consideration (e.g. the exchange of the land for an agreed price) for the main contract.

67. The celebrated epigram first appeared in the lecture on the *History of Contract* in The Common Law 215 (Howe ed. 1963): "Consideration is a form as much as a seal." He used it again, in the form in which it is quoted in the text, in Krell v. Codman, 154 Mass. 454, 28 N.E. 578 (1891), holding that a "voluntary covenant" made under seal in England by a lady who later died domiciled in Massachusetts which directed her executors to pay £2500 to the plaintiff was enforceable. Holmes assumed that the covenant was enforceable under English law and commented that it was "not contrary to the policy of our laws."

68. The reference is to 1 Williston, Contracts § 55 in the original (1920) edition.

69. 9 App. Cas. 605 (H.L. 1884).

70. Dean Ames had thoroughly reviewed the English cases (from 1455 on) in *Two Theories of Consideration*, 12 Harvard. L. Rev. 505, 521 *et seq.* (1899), concluding (at 527) that it was "greatly

to be deplored" that *Bagge v. Slade* (see note 74 *infra*) and other similar cases "were not brought to the attention of the court." In *Foakes v. Beer,* as will be presently explained in the text, principal reliance was placed on a dictum attributed to Lord Coke. Dean Ames commented: "Had Coke's real opinion . . . been made known to the Lords, it is not improbable that they would have followed it, instead of making him stand sponsor for a doctrine contrary to his declared convictions." (*Id.* at p. 527.) Corbin, following Ames, commented in a Note on *Part Payment of a Debt as Consideration for a Promise,* 17 Yale L.J. 470 (1908): "As is well known the rule [of *Foakes v. Beer*] is based on what is probably a misinterpretation of a dictum in *Pinnel's Case.* . . ." See further the discussion of *Foakes v. Beer* in 1A Corbin, Contracts § 175 (1963); 5A Corbin, Contracts § 1247 (1964); 6 Corbin, Contracts § 1281 (1962). Patterson, *An Apology for Consideration,* 48 Colum. L. Rev. 929, 936 *et seq.* (1958) follows the earlier commentators. For Williston's views, see text following note 76 *infra*.

71. History occasionally provides us with engaging coincidences. Holmes's first opinion after his appointment to the Massachusetts court, Weber v. Couch, 134 Mass. 26 (1883), involved a covenant by a creditor to release one of several joint debtors after a partial payment. The other debtors naturally argued that, under the well-known common law rule, the release of one effected the release of all. Holmes held against their contention on the ground that the covenant had been ineffective to release the debtor who had made the part payment. Without citation of authority of any kind he wrote: "A parol release of a judgment for money, in consideration of a payment of a smaller sum, is invalid at common law." It will be noted that *Weber v. Couch* (1883) antedated the decision of the House of Lords in *Foakes v. Beer* (1884).

72. For example, the Lord Chancellor made the point that nothing was done "on the receipt of the last payment, which could be tantamount to an acquittance, if the agreement did not previously bind her." (9 App. Cas. 605 at p. 611.) The reason why the

agreement would not have bound Mrs. Beer prior to full performance by Foakes was that the agreement constituted a so-called "executory accord" (an agreement by a creditor to accept a substituted performance from a debtor). The one thing that was thought to be clear about such accords at the time *Foakes v. Beer* was decided was that, so long as they remained executory, they were unenforceable. According to the common law slogan: "Upon an accord, no remedy lies." Actual performance of the accord, however, might result in "satisfaction." Foakes having paid and Mrs. Beer having accepted all the installments, their accord had been performed. But, as the Lord Chancellor pointed out, Mrs. Beer did not give Foakes anything in the nature of a release or "acquittance"—which would at least have resolved the factual ambiguity as to whether she had ever intended to release him from the payment of interest.

73. 5 Coke's Rep. 117 a, 77 Eng. Rep. 237 (1602).

74. Bagge v. Slade, 3 Bulst. 162, 81 Eng. Rep. 137 (1616). A and B were jointly liable on a bond. A paid the entire amount at B's request, B promising to reimburse A for half the payment. On B's refusal to keep his promise, A sued him and had judgment. "Here," said Coke, "is a good assumpsit grounded upon a good consideration. . . ." In discussing the case Coke is reported to have commented: "[I]f a man be bound to another by a bill in 1000 £ and he pays unto him 500 £ in discharge of this bill, the which he accepts of accordingly, and doth upon this assume and promise to deliver up unto him his said bill of 1000 £, this 500 £ is no satisfaction of the 1000 £, but yet this is good and sufficient to make a good promise, and upon a good consideration. . . ." Coke's thought seems to be that, while the part payment does not operate as a discharge, nevertheless the creditor's promise to release the debtor (or deliver up his bill) is enforceable ("a good assumpsit grounded upon a good consideration"). From this point of view the dictum in *Pinnel's*

132

Case may be taken as entirely consistent with Coke's more elaborate discussion of the point in *Bagge v. Slade.*

75. See Dean Ames's review of the cases in the article cited note 70 *supra.*

76. There was, as I have indicated (see note 70 *supra*), considerable dissent. There is, however, no question but that *Foakes v. Beer* (or its rule) became the leading case in this country as well as in England, Dean Ames to the contrary notwithstanding. For the orthodox English acceptance of the rule see 8 Holdsworth, A History of English Law 40 (2nd ed. 1937).

77. In the original (1920) edition, Williston, at this point, cited the article by Dean Ames (see note 70 *supra*), cases from Mississippi, New Hampshire, and Washington, the Indian Contract Act, a Canadian statute (British Columbia) and half a dozen American statutes.

78. 1 Williston, Contracts § 120 (1920). The passages quoted continue to appear without substantial change, except for the rearrangement of supporting footnote material, in the current (third) edition by Professor Jaeger.

79. The Common Law 5 ([1881] Howe ed. 1963).

80. See text at note 35 *supra.*

81. For the purpose of our discussion it is unnecessary to go into detailed documentation on the theories of "agreements to agree," "mutuality of obligation" and "illusory promises." See generally 1 Williston, Contracts §§ 37–49, 104–5A (3rd. ed. Jaeger, 1957).

82. Bailey v. Austrian, 19 Minn. 535 (Gil. 465) (1873) was long considered to be the leading case of this sort. Lavery, *The Doctrine of Bailey v. Austrian,* 10 Minn. L. Rev. 584 (1926) goes into the detail of the controversy.

83. The provisions of U.C.C. § 2-306 reflect the eventual solution. See the materials collected in Kessler & Gilmore, Contracts—Cases and Materials (1970), ch. 4, § 10 (Requirement Contracts and Mutuality).

II. Development

84. See text following note 61 *supra*.

85. 2 Hurl & C. 906, 159 Eng. Rep. 375 (Ex. 1864).

86. The three judges were Pollack, Martin, and Pigott—none of them known to fame as an expounder of commercial law.

87. The date of the case (1864) suggests a plausible explanation of why there should have been a break in the price of cotton in English markets at this time. During the early years of our Civil War, the effective Northern naval blockade prevented cotton from being shipped out of Southern ports. After the capture of New Orleans and other ports by Northern forces the Lincoln administration confiscated large stocks of cotton which were sold for export. I assume that American cotton could be sold in England more cheaply than Indian cotton of comparable quality because of reduced transportation costs.

88. On "to arrive" see U.C.C. § 12-324 ("No Arrival, No Sale" Term). According to the Official Comment: "The 'no arrival, no sale' term [equivalent to "to arrive"] in a 'destination' overseas contract leaves risk of loss on the seller but gives him an exemption from liability for non-delivery."

On "ex Peerless" see U.C.C. § 2-322 (Delivery "Ex-Ship"). According to the Official Comment: "Delivery need not be made from any particular vessel under a clause calling for delivery 'ex ship' even though a vessel on which shipment is to be made originally is named in the contract, unless the agreement by appropriate language, restricts the clause to delivery from a named vessel."

Thus, under the Code formulation, Milward need not even have made the concession that the cotton had to arrive on a ship called Peerless.

89. For Mellish's adherence to the consensus ad idem (or "meeting of the minds") idea after he became a judge, see the discussion of his opinion in *Dickinson v. Dodds* in the preceding lecture, text following note 61 *supra*.

90. See the text following note 61 *supra*.

91. Kyle v. Kavanaugh, 103 Mass. 356 (1869). It is one of the mysteries of the legal literature that every English-speaking lawyer knows *Raffles v. Wichelhaus* while no one has even heard of *Kyle v. Kavanaugh*. The case involved a contract for the sale of land located on "Prospect Street" in Waltham. In the seller's action for the price, one of the buyer's pleas was that there were two "Prospect Streets" in Waltham; the seller had offered to convey land located on one of the Prospect Streets but the buyer had intended to buy land located on the other Prospect Street. In affirming a judgment for the defendant-buyer, Morton, J., commented, with respect to the "two Prospect Streets plea": "The instructions given [by the trial judge] were, in substance, that, if the defendant was negotiating for one thing and the plaintiff was selling another thing, and their minds did not agree as to the subject matter of the sale, there would be no contract by which the defendant would be bound, though there was no fraud on the part of the plaintiff. This ruling is in accordance with the elementary principles of the law of contracts, and was correct." (103 Mass. at 359-60.) The only authority cited was Spurr v. Benedict, 99 Mass. 463 (1868), which had decreed rescission of a land contract for non-fraudulent misrepresentation by the seller about the acreage and quality of the land conveyed.

In *Kyle v. Kavanaugh* the mistake as to the location of the land was, unquestionably, "material" and, it may be noted, the seller apparently lost nothing except his anticipated profit.

92. Boulton v. Jones, 2 H. & N. 564, 157 Eng. Rep. 232 (Ex. 1857) (Pollock and Martin, two of the judges in *Raffles v. Wichelhaus*, see note 86 *supra*, also sat in *Boulton v. Jones*); Boston Ice Co. v. Potter, 123 Mass. 28 (1877). In both cases C had taken over B's business and furnished the goods without notifying A of the change of ownership. The opinions wrestle ambiguously with a good many peripheral issues (set-off and assignment) but I think that the cases can fairly be taken as illustrations of the attitude next referred to in the text. Much of the commentary on the two cases, which has been extensive (see Kessler & Gilmore, Contracts—Cases and Materials 44 Note [1970]), assumes that the plaintiffs lost their contractual actions but would have been entitled to some form of quasi-contractual recovery. I see no reason to believe that either court would have granted any kind of relief. Indeed Bramwell, B., in *Boulton v. Jones*, remarked: "As to the difficulty that the defendants need not pay anybody, I do not see why they should, unless they have made a contract either express or implied."

93. Why?

94. Holmes, The Common Law 242 ([1881] Howe ed. 1963). In his footnote Holmes, after giving the citation for *Raffles v. Wichelhaus*, adds: "Cf. *Kyle v. Kavanaugh*, 103 Mass. 356, 347." On *Kyle v. Kavanaugh*, see note 91 *supra*. Evidently the analysis which Holmes offered was meant to explain the "true ground of . . . decision" in both cases.

95. See the analysis of *Stilk v. Myrick, Dickinson v. Dodds*, and *Foakes v. Beer*, text following note 43 *supra*.

96. See his comment about "the whole doctine of contract" being "formal and external," quoted in the text at note 41 *supra*.

On this aspect of Holmesian jurisprudence, see Mark Howe's admirable introduction to his edition of *The Common Law*, particularly at p. xx *et seq.*, as well as the chapters which are devoted to *The Common Law* in the second volume of Howe's biography of Holmes, *The Proving Years* (1963).

97. 13 Williston, Contracts 32–34, 36 § 153b (Confusion Concerning Nature of Assent in Contract) (1970). For other illustrations of Williston's version of objectivism see (in volume 1 of the treatise) § 20 (Genuineness of Consent), § 21 (Intent to Contract), § 95 (When Mistake Will Prevent Formation of Contract); one might indeed cite the entire treatise, *passim*.

One of the best known judicial expressions of the objective theory is by Learned Hand (who had been a student of Williston's and acknowledged the great influence which Williston had had on his thinking) in Hotchkiss v. National City Bank of New York, 200 Fed. 287, 293 (S.D.N.Y. 1911): "A contract has, strictly speaking, nothing to do with the personal, or individual, intent of the parties. A contract is an obligation attached by the mere force of law to certain acts of the parties, usually words, which ordinarily accompany and represent a known intent." (Williston, in the section from which the quotation in the text is taken, approvingly quotes the *Hotchkiss* opinion, which he refers to as "classic.")

For a later judicial attack on the excesses of "objectivism," see the extraordinary law review article disguised as a concurring opinion by Judge Frank in Ricketts v. Pennsylvania R. Co., 153 F. 2d 757, 760 (2d Cir. 1946). (The majority opinion in *Ricketts* was by Judge Learned Hand.)

98. Text following note 35 *supra*.

99. That Holmes was consciously engaged in such a "narrowing" process is entirely clear. The entire lecture on Void and Voidable Contracts in *The Common Law* is devoted to the argument that excuses from liability such as mistake, fraud, misrepresentation, and so on should be confined within the narrowest possible

range. His explanation of the "true ground of . . . decision" in *Raffles v. Wichelhaus* has been quoted in the text at note 94 *supra*. In the immediately following passage of the lecture, he went on to suggest that the doctrine or rule of *Raffles* applied only to the case of a "proper name" which unexpectedly turned out to have more than one meaning. For a comparably narrow reading of *Raffles*, see the extremely interesting article by Professor Young, *Equivocation in the Making of Agreements*, 64 Colum. L. Rev. 619 (1964).

100. See text following note 25 *supra*.

101. Aleyn 26, 82 Eng. Rep. 897; Style 47, 82 Eng. Rep. 519 (K.B. 1647).

102. The odd reference to "alien enemies" is explained by the fact that Prince Rupert was German by birth. The sister of King Charles I had married a German prince and Rupert was their son. Rupert was, thus, Charles's nephew; he served as commander of the royal cavalry during the Civil Wars in England.

103. Adams v. Nichols, 19 Pick. (Mass. 1837) 275, 276.

104. According to the report in Aleyn (see note 101 *supra*): "[W]here the law creates a duty or charge, and the party is disabled to perform it without any default in him, and hath no remedy over, there the law will excuse him. . . . [B]ut when the party by his own contract creates a duty or charge upon himself, he is bound to make it good, if he may, notwithstanding any accident by inevitable necessity, because he might have provided against it in his contract."

The report of the case in Style has no analogue to the second sentence quoted above. According to Style, the decision went on this ground: "[I]f the tenant for years covenant to pay rent, though the lands let him be surrounded with water, yet he is chargeable with the rent, much more here." The analogy of the land surrounded by water also appears in the Aleyn report.

105. Monk v. Cooper, 2 Strange 763, 93 Eng. Rep. 833 (K.B. 1723). On the seventeenth century idea of the "independence" of mutual covenants, see also Nichols v. Raynbred, Hobart 88, 80 Eng. Rep. 238 (C.P. 1615): Pordage v. Cole, 1 Wms. Saunders 319h, 85 Eng. Rep. 449 (K.B. 1669).

106. This is the explanation of the case which was put forward by Professor Corbin; see 6 Corbin, Contracts § 1322 (1962).

107. 2 Wms. Saunders 420, 85 Eng. Rep. 1233 (K.B. 1684).

108. See, e.g., 1 Story, Equity Jurisprudence § 101 (1836); School Trustees of Trenton v. Bennett, 27 N.J.L. 513 (1859).

109. *Paradine* is still cited to this proposition in our own day. See e.g., Simpson, Handbook of the Law of Contracts 359 (2d ed. 1965); Berman, *Excuse for Nonperformance in the Light of Contract Practices in International Trade*, 63 Colum. L. Rev. 1413, 1417 (1963).

110. An excellent example of the nineteenth century treatment of the "plaintiff in default" situation is the opinion by Comstock, J., in Smith v. Brady, 17 N.Y. 173 (1858). In the course of his opinion Comstock states the following hypothetical: "If A. should agree to plow the field of B., consisting of twenty acres, at a given price for the whole service, or at so much per acre to be paid when the service is done, and after plowing nineteen acres should abandon the contract, he can recover nothing for his work." (17 N.Y. at 188.) Comstock includes a savage criticism of Britton v. Turner, 6 N.H. 481 (1834) in which an agricultural laborer who had been engaged for a year but quit without excuse after serving nine months was allowed to recover nine-twelfths of the amount which would have been due him at the end of the year. Indeed the New Hampshire case seems to have been regarded as aberrational by most nineteenth century commentators. See further the opinion

by Folger, J., in Laurence v. Miller, 86 N.Y. 131 (1881): it would be "ill doctrine" to "declare that a party may violate his agreement, and make an infraction of it by himself a cause of action." (86 N.Y. at 140.)

111. On the apparently promising eighteenth century beginnings of such theories of excuse and their withering on the vine in the course of the nineteenth century, see Dawson, *Economic Duress—An Essay in Perspective*, 45 Mich. L. Rev. 253 (1947).

112. Text at note 42 *supra*.

113. 9 Ex. 341, 156 Eng. Rep. 145 (1854).

114. According to the report of the case, the plaintiffs had claimed damages of £300.

115. According to Alderson but not, as all first year law students learn, according to the headnote in the case report which says that the defendants were told "that the mill was stopped, that the shaft must be delivered immediately, and that a special entry, if necessary, must be made to hasten its delivery."

116. The Common Law 236–37 ([1881] Howe ed. 1963). The case about the sawmill machinery to which Holmes referred approvingly was British Columbia and Vancouver's Island Spar, Lumber and Saw-Mill Co., Limited v. Nettleship, L.R. 3 C.P. 499 (1868). Holmes's opinion in Globe Refining Co. v. Landa Cotton Oil Co., 190 U.S. 540 (1903), restated the same theoretical position without any change of substance and indeed in language borrowed from the passage quoted in the text. The phrase which Holmes quotes at the end of the passage is from the opinion by Willes, J., in the *Columbia Saw-Mill* case.

117. See, for example, Mayne, The Law of Damages 10 (2d ed. 1872) and the opinion of Blackburn, J., in Elbinger Actien-

Gesellschaft etc. v. Armstrong, L.R. 9 Q.B. 473 (1874). Blackburn, author of a celebrated treatise on the law of sales, was one of the leading commercial lawyers (and judges) of the period.

118. See text following note 12 *supra*.

119. 2 W. Bl. 1078, 96 Eng. Rep. 635 (C.P. 1776).

120. The rule on money contracts is usually traced back to Robinson v. Bland, 2 Burr. 1077, 97 Eng. Rep. 717 (1760) (per Lord Mansfield).

121. The sales rule first appears in late eighteenth century cases which involved transactions on the London stock exchange (a special situation in which the rule made [and makes] excellent sense). The rule was generalized as being applicable to all sales of personal property in Gainsford v. Carroll, 2 B. & C. 624, 107 Eng. Rep. 516 (K.B. 1828). The assumption which underlies the "contract and market" rule is evidently the same as the assumption that underlies the money rule—namely, that substitute or replacement goods are universally and instantly available." In the real world (as distinguished from the stock exchange) that is simply not true, which is the reason why I have described the rule as one which is non-compensatory and does not protect the expectation interest. Much of the commentary on the rule assumes, contrary to my own analysis, that it is compensatory (or at least is meant to be compensatory) and that giving plaintiff the contract-and-market differential is the same thing as giving him profits or his expectation. For an example of that approach to the rule, see Holmes's opinion in the *Globe Refining Co.* case, cited note 116 *supra*.

122. Most of the commentary on *Hadley* has emphasized what might be called its "negative" aspect—that is, its usefulness as a device for controlling large damage verdicts by irresponsible juries since, with *Hadley*, all damage questions become matters of

law, reviewable on appeal. Unquestionably this aspect of *Hadley* exists and is of great importance. See the discussion of the "objective theory of contract" earlier in this lecture, where the point was made that one of the basic predispositions of the general theory of contract was to resolve "questions originally perceived as questions of fact . . . into questions of law." The "negative" aspect of *Hadley* was entirely consistent with this predisposition. But Alderson's formula, as the earlier, hostile critics correctly perceived, had its affirmative aspect as well which, if taken seriously, could open a Pandora's box of large recoveries for so-called "consequential damages." On the extent to which Pandora's box has been opened in our own century, see the text following note 227 *infra*.

123. For Holmes's insistence on the difference between damage recovery in tort and damage recovery in contract see the first part of the passage from *The Common Law* set out in the text at note 116 *supra*.

124. Holmes returned to this idea (which he sometimes referred to as his "bad man" theory of law) over and over throughout his career. He may have given it its most eloquent statement in his address *The Path of the Law* (in Collected Legal Papers 167, 170 *et. seq.* [1920]). In his opinion in the *Globe Refining Co.* case, cited note 116 *supra*, he wrote: "If a contract is broken, the measure of damages generally is the same, whatever the cause of the breach. . . . The motive for the breach commonly is immaterial in an action on the contract." (190 U.S. at 544, 547.) The idea surfaces in a variety of contexts throughout the lectures on *The Common Law*.

125. Professor Allan Farnsworth concludes his remarkable article on *Legal Remedies for Breach of Contract*, 70 Colum. L. Rev. 1145 (1970) with the observation (at 1216): "All in all, our system of legal remedies for breach of contract, heavily influenced by the economic philosophy of free enterprise, showed a marked solicitude for men who do not keep their promises."

142

III. Decline and Fall

126. See text following note 24 *supra*.

127. On July 26, 1966, Lord Gardiner announced, on behalf of the House of Lords, that "Their Lordships . . . propose . . . to modify their present practice and, while treating former decisions of this House as normally binding, to depart from a previous decision when it appears right to do so." See [1966] 3 All Eng. L.R. 77.

128. Fuller & Perdue, *The Reliance Interest in Contract Damages*, 46 Yale L.J. 52, 373 (1936).

129. Kessler & Fine, *"Culpa in Contrahendo," Bargaining in Good Faith and Freedom of Contract: A Comparative Study*, 77 Harv. L. Rev. 401 (1964). The principle referred to in the text has long been overtly recognized in German law under the *culpa in contrahendo* rubric. Professor Kessler demonstrates that the same principle can be deduced from a study of the American case law, although the principle has never been overtly recognized in American jurisprudence.

130. "Ignorance is the best of law reformers." Holmes, The Common Law 64 ([1881] Howe ed. 1963).

131. 1 Corbin, Contracts § 109 (1963).

132. See text at note 41 *supra*.

133. Gilmore, *Legal Realism: Its Cause and Cure*, 70 Yale L.J. 1037 (1961).

134. *The Restatement of Contracts* was first published in 1932. On the personal and intellectual relationship between Williston and Corbin, see the moving notice which Corbin (then nearly 90) wrote for the issue of the *Harvard Law Review* which was dedicated to Williston's memory; Corbin, *Samuel Williston*, 76 Harv. L. Rev. 1327 (1963).

135. In the following pages I reproduce the substance of conversations which I had with Professor Corbin during the early 1950s. Thus the conversations themselves took place twenty years ago and the events which Professor Corbin was describing had taken place twenty or thirty years before that. Obviously there is bound to be a certain amount of slippage between what really happened and this second-hand reconstruction of what happened.

136. Of particular interest in this connection is Corbin's analysis of the Cardozo contract opinions in the extraordinary tribute to Cardozo which was published jointly by the *Columbia Law Review*, the *Harvard Law Review*, and the *Yale Law Journal* in 1939; see, Corbin, *Mr. Justice Cardozo and the Law of Contracts*, 39 Colum. L. Rev. 56; 52 Harv. L. Rev. 408; 48 Yale L.J. 426.

137. Outlet Embroidery Co. v. Derwent Mills, 254 N.Y. 179, 172 N.E. 462 (1930) is a well-known example of this approach: "The letters between plaintiff and defendant were from one merchant to another. They are to be read as business men would read them, and only as a last resort are to be thrown out as meaningless futilities. . . . In the transactions of business life, sanity of end and aim is at least a presumption, albeit subject to be rebutted. . . . If literalness is sheer absurdity, we are to seek some other meaning whereby reason will be instilled and absurdity avoided." (254 N.Y. at 183.) Cardozo was not always a model of consistency. In The Sun Printing & Publishing Assn. v. Remington Paper & Power Co., Inc., 235 N.Y. 338, 139 N.E. 470 (1923), he wrote the opinion for the majority of the court (two judges dissented) holding a contract for the sale of newsprint void for indefiniteness because of an insufficiently precise price term. Even Corbin found the *Sun Printing* decision "surprising." "Was Cardozo," he speculated, "less moved to cure defects in the work of the well-paid lawyers of two rich corporations" than he would have been in most other cases? (Corbin, *op. cit. supra* note 136, 39 Colum. L. Rev. at 58.)

138. See, e.g., Cohen & Sons v. Lurie Woolen Co., 232 N.Y. 112, 133 N.E. 370 (1921).

139. The most celebrated example of this technique is Wood v. Lucy, Lady Duff-Gordon, 222 N.Y. 88, 118 N.E. 214 (1917). Another is Moran v. Standard Oil Co., 211 N.Y. 187, 105 N.E. 217 (1914).

140. DeCicco v. Schweizer, 221 N.Y. 431, 117 N.E. 807 (1917). Corbin, in the article cited at note 136 *supra*, commenting that "No one can doubt the soundness of this decision" (or its "justice"), demonstrates at some length that it cannot be squared with the by then orthodox bargain theory of consideration (39 Colum. L. Rev. at 61 *et. seq.*).

141. Allegheny College v. National Chautauqua Bank, 246 N.Y. 369, 377, 159 N.E. 173 (1927).

142. On causa and the close approach to such a theory by the English courts during Lord Mansfield's tenure on the bench, see note 32 *supra* and the text at that point.

143. See the text at and following note 36 *supra*.

144. Text at note 34 *supra*.

145. At common law the "estoppel" or "estoppel in pais" idea was originally restricted to misrepresentations about existing facts. If I tell you that something is so (when it is not so) and you reasonably rely on my statement to your detriment, I will not be heard, in the resulting litigation, to deny the truth of what I said. In the "equitable estoppel" and "promissory estoppel" cases the concept was broadened to include statements, assurances or promises relating to future events or future conduct. (The term "promissory estoppel" gradually won out over the term "equitable estoppel" which had been used with some frequency in the earlier cases.) Thus if I have promised to do something and you have reasonably relied on my promise to your detriment, I will be estopped

to deny liability, even though it is clear as crystal that I had no intention of "bargaining" for your detriment. In this way "promissory estoppel" served as the escape from the bargain theory of consideration. It was, of course, only courts which had accepted the bargain theory of consideration in the first place which then had to develop theories of promissory estoppel to get out of their self-imposed dilemma. Promissory estoppel theory was, for this reason, not necessary and was not resorted to in New York (or for that matter in England where Holmesian bargain theory was never taken seriously). Cardozo's opinion in the *Allegheny College* case, note 141 *supra*, was essentially a demonstration of why the broad New York consideration theory made promissory estoppel an unnecessary and undesirable refinement.

146. Corbin collects the cases in chapter 8 ("Reliance on a Promise as Ground for Enforcement") of his treatise.

147. The illustrations are:

1. A promises B not to foreclose for a specified time, a mortgage which A holds on B's land. B thereafter makes improvements on the land. A's promise is binding.

2. A promises B to pay him an annuity during B's life. B thereupon resigns a profitable employment, as A expected that he might. B receives the annuity for some years, in the meantime becoming disqualified from again obtaining good employment. A's promise is binding.

3. A promises B that if B will go to college and complete his course he will give him $5000. B goes to college and has nearly completed his course, when A notifies him of an intention to revoke the promise. A's promise is binding.

4. A promises B $5000, knowing that B desires that sum

for the purchase of Blackacre. Induced thereby, B se-
cures without any payment an option to buy Blackacre. A then tells B that he withdraws his promise.
A's promise is not binding.

Without engaging in extended commentary, we may note that
Illustration 4 evidently defined the outer limits of § 90: no recovery for what might be called disappointed expectations. Illustrations 2 and 3 involved non-commercial gift promises, see the text
at note 150 *infra*. The scope of Illustration 1 is difficult, indeed impossible, to determine, since we are not told who A and B were or
why A promised not to foreclose the mortgage.

148. On third party beneficiaries, see chapter 6 §§ 133–47
(Contractual Rights of Persons not Parties to the Contract). On
anticipatory breach, see §§ 318–24. On excuse by reason of impossibility or frustration, cf. § 288 (frustration) with chapter 14 § 454–69
(Impossibility). On plaintiff in default, see § 357.

149. It would be a waste of time to collect citations to document this and the preceding sentence in the text. See the relevant
sections of the two treatises.

150. James Baird Co. v. Gimbel Bros., 64 F. 2d 344 (2d Cir.
1933). Much of the early law review commentary was to the same
effect. See Boyer, *Promissory Estoppel: Principle from Precedents*,
50 Mich. L. Rev. 639, 873 (1952); Shattuck, *Gratuitous Promises—
A New Writ*, 35 Mich. L. Rev. 908 (1937). Fuller & Perdue, *The Reliance Interest in Contract Damages*, 46 Yale L.J. 52, 373 (1936)
made the same assumption as to § 90, although the point of the
Fuller & Perdue article (see text at note 128 *supra*) was that the reliance interest had received much more protection at common law
than had been generally assumed.

151. For this development see Henderson, *Promissory Estoppel and Traditional Contract Doctrine*, 78 Yale L.J. 343 (1969);

Comment, *Once More Into the Breach: Promissory Estoppel and Traditional Damage Doctrine,* 37 U. of Chi. L. Rev. 559 (1970).

152. See, e.g., N. Litterio & Co., Inc. v. Glassman Construction Co., Inc., 319 F. 2d 736 (D.C. Cir. 1963). The court, although it found that no "contract" had been entered into, remanded the case for further proceedings on whether there might, nevertheless, be liability on promissory estoppel theory. In this context Judge Fahy commented: "The issue as to the Statute of Frauds is no longer germaine in light of our holding that no contract was created." (319 F. 2d at 740, note 9.)

153. For an excellent discussion and a collection of the recent cases, see the Chicago. Comment cited note 151 *supra.*

154. See text at and following note 133 *supra.*

155. 1 Restatement, Contracts at xi (1932).

156. Dean Lewis's approach seems to have been in direct descent from Langdell's. See the passage from the introduction to Langdell's casebook on contracts quoted in the text at note 22 *supra,* particularly Langdell's reference to "fundamental legal doctrines."

157. See the Introductions by the late Judge Goodrich (then Director of the Institute) to the *Restatement (Second) of Agency* (1958) and *Restatement (Second) of Trusts* (1959)—the first two entries in the new series.

158. It should be noted that the "official" position of the Institute, at least during the early years of the Second Restatement project, was that nothing had really changed, that things were much as they always had been, and that the good law of the 1930s was still the good law of the 1950s. Thus, in his Introduction to *Agency (Second)* (1958) Judge Goodrich said: "Few of the rules laid down in the first edition have been changed." And the following year in the Introduction to *Trusts (Second)* he added: "There will

not be very much here which is contrary to what was said in the First Edition." However, the Introduction to *Conflict of Laws (Second)* (1971), by Professor Herbert Wechsler, who had succeeded Judge Goodrich as Director, struck a different note. After commenting that "the new work is far more than a current version of the old . . . what is presented here is a fresh treatment of the subject," he went on: "It is a treatment that takes full account of the enormous change in dominant judicial thought respecting conflicts problems that has taken place in relatively recent years. The essence of that change has been the jettisoning of a multiplicity of rigid rules in favor of standards of greater flexibility, according sensitivity in judgment to important values that were formerly ignored. Such a transformation in the corpus of the law reduces certitude as well as certainty, posing a special problem in the process of restatement. Its solution lies in candid recognition that black-letter formulation must often consist of open-ended standards. . . . The result [in *Conflicts (Second)*] presents a striking contrast to the first Restatement in which dogma was so thoroughly enshrined." We may accept the points that the *First Restatement of Conflicts* "enshrined dogma" to an unusual degree and that there has been a great deal of activity, both judicial and academic, in the field in recent years. Nevertheless, Professor Wechsler's recognition of the need for "open-ended standards" seems quite as applicable to Contracts as it does to Conflicts, despite the fact that the *First Restatement of Contracts* was non-dogmatic to a degree bordering, as I have suggested, on "schizophrenia" (see text at note 134 *supra*).

159. 1 Gilmore, Security Interests in Personal Property 298 (1965).

160. See text following note 133 *supra*.

161. Justice Frankfurter addressed one of the annual meetings of the Institute in the late 1940s. Evidently no one had told the Justice of the sudden change of course since, to the

general bewilderment, he paid tribute, eloquently and at length, to the Institute's single-minded devotion to the common law process and its refusal to have anything to do with statutes.

162. We should not overlook what might be called the principle of institutional inertia: any institution seeks to continue in existence although its reason for existence has vanished. The Institute's 1952 decision to do over the Restatements may also have been occasioned by a grant which it received from the Mellon Foundation (see the Introduction to the several Restatements [Second]). Another principle of institutional life is that, if money is available, it must be spent.

163. At the moment of writing, the Restatement of Contracts (Second) has not been completed. Between 1964 and 1971 six "Tentative Drafts" appeared. (The "Drafts" did not represent successive revisions; each Draft presented new material.) The Reporter was Professor Robert Braucher of the Harvard Law School (now Mr. Justice Braucher of the Supreme Judicial Court of Massachusetts). Professor E. Allen Farnsworth of the Columbia Law School has succeeded Justice Braucher as Reporter (Tentative Draft No. 7, 1972). The sections of Contracts (Second) with which we shall be concerned appeared in Tentative Draft No. 2 (1965).

164. See text preceding note 135 *supra*.

165. Until his death in 1967 Professor Corbin served as "Consultant" to the Reporter, Professor Braucher. On the "Corbinization" of the § 75 Comment, cf. 1 Corbin, Contracts §§ 109, 110 (1963): "Who can now read all the reports of cases dealing with the law of consideration for informal promises, stating the reasons deemed sufficient for enforcing such promises, laying down the doctrines and constructing the definitions? Certainly not the writer of this volume. He has merely read enough of them to feel well assured that the reasons for enforcing informal promises are many, that the doctrine of consideration is many

doctrines, that no definition can rightly be set up as the one and only correct definition, and that the law of contract is an evolutionary product that has changed with time and circumstance and that must ever continue so to change. . . .

". . . In each new case, the question for the court is 'should this promise be enforced.' Its problem is not merely to determine mechanically, or logically, whether it falls within Professor Wiseacre's statement of the doctrine of consideration or complies with some commonly repeated definition. This is not to say that the Professor's statement or restatement, or the learned judge's dictum, can be safely disregarded." I dare say that the identity of "Professor Wiseacre" is sufficiently obvious; I assume that the "learned judge" is Holmes. For Corbin on Holmes, see text at and following note 131 *supra*.

166. The "concession" in the Comment immediately followed the typically Holmesian statement: "The fact that the promisee relies on the promise to his injury, or that the promisor gains some advantage therefrom, does not establish consideration without the element of bargain or agreed exchange. . . ." For Holmes on benefit and detriment, see text at and following note 35 *supra*. The sequence of sections (§ 85–94) referred to in the Comment was captioned "Informal Contracts without Assent or Consideration" and took up such things as promises to pay debts barred by a Statute of Limitations or discharged in bankruptcy, promises to perform a "voidable duty," and a couple of other exotic trivia which (except for § 90) are of little interest or importance.

167. See Illustration 3, note 147 *supra*.

168. Indeed the relevant comment (b) has been rewritten in terms which clearly echo the celebrated passage from *The Common Law* quoted in the text at note 35 *supra*.

169. See note 147 *supra* and the accompanying text.

170. The four original illustrations (note 147 *supra*) have been retained, albeit with a couple of somewhat confusing changes. Illustration 1 (renumbered 2) is unchanged except for the addition of the statement that the promise "may be enforced by denial of foreclosure before the time has elapsed." In Illustration 2 (renumbered 4) the reference to the employee's "in the meantime becoming disqualified from again obtaining good employment" has been deleted and statements added that the employee has been employed by the employer for 40 years and that the promised "pension" is $200 per month. In Illustration 3 (renumbered 1) a new element has been added—that B, at the time when A attempts to revoke, has "borrow[ed] and spen[t] more than $5000 for college expenses." The revised illustration also explicitly comments that the promise is "binding . . . without regard to whether [B's] performance was 'bargained for and given in exchange for' the promise under § 75 [§ 71]." Illustration 4 (renumbered 5) is unchanged— from which we may perhaps conclude that "disappointed expectations" (see note 137 *supra*) are not meant to be protected under revised § 90 any more than they were under the original.

It is hard to know what, if anything, should be made of these changes. The addition to Illustration 1 (renumbered 2) appears to be meaningless. Illustration 2 (renumbered 4) may have been rewritten to conform the hypothetical to the facts of Feinberg v. Pfeiffer Co., 322 S.W. 2d 163 (Mo. App. 1959) on which, according to the Reporter's Notes (T.D. No. 2 at p. 175), the Illustration is now based. The change in Illustration 3 (renumbered 1) presumably reflects the substantive change in the text of revised § 90 which is next discussed in the text and may be taken to mean that if B's reliance expenses had been less than $5000 his recovery would be reduced accordingly. See text at note 171 *infra*.

171. The section as revised also protects action or forbearance "on the part of . . . a third person" as well as "on the part of the promisee"—which presumably clears up a point on which the original § 90 was thought to have been unclear.

172. The text of original § 90 was, to say the least, unclear on the "limitation" of remedy. In discussion of the proposed section at the 1926 meeting of the Institute, Mr. Coudert, a distinguished member of the New York bar, put to Professor Williston a hypothetical case in which Uncle promised Nephew $1000 to buy a car and Nephew, in reliance, bought a car for $500. Was Nephew, Mr. Coudert inquired, entitled to recover $500? Or $1000? Professor Williston uncompromisingly took the position that Nephew's recovery should be $1000: "Either the promise is binding or it is not. If the promise is binding it has to be enforced as it is made." (4 A.L.I. Proceedings (1926) 98-99, 103-104.) The Coudert-Williston colloquy found its way into the law review literature and the contracts casebooks. Corbin took a quite different tack from Williston's; see 1A Corbin, Contracts (1963) § 205. See further Fuller & Perdue, *The Reliance Interest in Contract Damages*, 46 Yale L.J. 52, 373 (1936). Professor Fuller reproduced the Coudert-Williston exchange at p. 64. He commented (at p. 401) that Williston's result might have been deduced "from the systematics of the Restatement" taken as a whole but Professor Fuller did not think highly of the Restatement's "systematics."

173. Restatement of Contracts (Second), Tentative Draft No. 2 (1965) at 165-66 [Restatement of Contracts (Second), Official Text (1981) at 242-43 (Comment a)].

174. He hath put down the mighty from their seats
And hath exalted them of low degree.

175. See text at note 150 *supra*.

176. See note 152 *supra* and the accompanying text. Conceivably illustration 14 (B promises A that he will not build on his own land in such a way as to obstruct the view from land which A, relying, then purchases) could be read to mean that a Statute of Frauds defense is not available in § 90 action.

177. For an illuminating discussion of the treatment of Good

Samaritans and others who engage in disinterested benevolence, see Dawson, *"Negotiorum Gestio"*: *The Altruistic Intermeddler*, 74 Harv. L. Rev. 817, 1073 (1961). Professor Dawson concluded that Anglo-American law has been less generous in rewarding Good Samaritans than have most of the European civil law systems. See also Wade, *Restitution for Benefits Conferred without Request*, 19 Vand. L. Rev. 1183 (1966). Dean Wade's article and the article by Professor Lee cited in note 182 *infra* appeared in an excellent *Symposium on Restitution* which included a number of interesting contributions.

178. See note 110 *supra* and the accompanying text.

179. The quantum meruit idea makes its appearance as far back as Britton v. Turner, 6 N.H. 481 (1834) (the case about the agricultural laborer who quit after nine months). The New Hampshire court held that plaintiff could have a quantum meruit recovery for the time he had worked, even though it appeared that he had quit wilfully and without excuse. On almost identical facts the New York and Massachusetts courts had denied recovery: Lantry v. Parks, 8 Cowen 63 (N.Y. Sup. Ct. 1827); Stark v. Parker, 2 Pick, 149 (Mass. 1824). As suggested in note 110 *supra*, the New Hampshire case was looked on as aberrational throughout the nineteenth century.

180. This was the approach taken in Cotnam v. Wisdom, 83 Ark. 601, 104 S.W. 164 (1907): physician who had rendered services to an unconscious man who died without regaining consciousness *held* entitled to recover the value of his services from the estate. To the same effect, *in re* Crisan Estate, 362 Mich. 569, 107 N.W. 2d 907 (1961).

181. A celebrated example of this approach is Jacob & Youngs, Inc. v. Kent, 230 N.Y. 239, 129 N.E. 889 (1921) (per Cardozo, J.). It is instructive to compare Cardozo's rhetoric in *Jacob & Youngs* with the rhetoric of Comstock, J. in *Smith v. Brady* (1858), note 110 *supra*.

182. Freedman v. The Rector, Warden & Vestrymen, 37 Cal. 2d 16, 230 P. 2d 629 (1951). See also Amtorg Trading Corp. v. Miehle Printing Press & Mfg. Co., 206 F. 2d 103 (2d Cir. 1953) in which Clark, J., (who was *Erie*-bound) expressed the belief or hope that the New York Court of Appeals, if the occasion presented itself, would reverse the nineteenth-century New York rule illustrated by such cases as *Smith v. Brady*, note 110 *supra*. In Proctor & Gamble Distributing Co. v. Lawrence American Field Warehousing Corp., 16 N.Y. 2d 344, 213 N.E. 2d 873 (1965), Van Voorhis, J., commented that U.C.C. § 2-718(2) had reversed the old New York rule as to contracts for the sale of goods. The Court of Appeals has not, so far, chosen to deal with the plaintiff in default problem in general terms. Lee, *The Plaintiff in Default*, 19 Vand. L. Rev. 102 (1966), after reviewing the cases for the 1950–65 period, concluded that cases like *Freedman* and *Amtorg* were still in the minority. *Restatement* (*First*) § 357 dealt with Restitution in Favor of a Plaintiff Who is Himself in Default in what I have characterized as a "curiously fudged or blurred" fashion (text at and following note 148 *supra*).

183. I assume that, as a matter of statutory construction, subsection (2) is to be taken on a gloss on "to the extent necessary to prevent injustice" in subsection (1).

184. Illustration 1 to § 89A [§ 86], based on, per the Reporter's Note, Mills v. Wyman, 3 Pick. 207 (Mass. 1826).

185. Illustration 7 to § 89A [§ 86], based on, per the Reporter's Note, Webb v. McGowin, 232 Ala. 374, 168 So. 199 (1936).

186. Illustration 6 to § 89A [§ 86], based on, per the Reporter's Note, Boothe v. Fitzpatrick, 36 Vt. 681 (1864).

187. In *Mills v. Wyman*, note 184 *supra*, the son died while still in the Good Samaritan's care. Illustration 1 to § 89A [§ 86] does not use this fact. I do not know whether the omission was purposeful or inadvertent.

188. See text at note 134 *supra*.

Henderson, *Promises Grounded in the Past: The Idea of Unjust Enrichment and the Law of Contracts*, 57 Va. L. Rev. 1115 (1971) discusses the § 89A [§ 86] formulation and elaborately analyzes the case law background. Professor Henderson's point is that ideas of unjust enrichment and "moral obligation" have played a greater role in the case law than the modest walk-on part that has conventionally been assigned to them. In this respect his article follows in the tradition of the articles by Professors Fuller and Kessler discussed in the text at notes 128 and 129 *supra*. Professor Henderson's remarkable article came to my attention just as copy for this book was going to the printer; if I had known it earlier, I would have made more use of it.

In Braucher, *Freedom of Contract and the Second Restatement*, 78 Yale L. J. 598 (1969), the then Reporter for *Restatement* (*Second*) (see note 163 *supra*) commented that § 89A [§ 86] "probably has more theoretical interest than practical significance," adding that "the new section [§ 89A] [§ 86] states a principle rather than a rule and fairly bristles with unspecific concepts" (at pp. 604, 605).

189. See Lecture 2, text following note 44 to end of chapter.

190. Lingenfelder v. The Wainwright Brewing Co., 103 Mo. 578, 15 S.W. 844 (1890) is a classical example.

191. See, e.g., Schwartzreich v. Bauman-Basch, Inc., 231 N.Y. 196, 131 N.E. 887 (1921) (Modifications); Fuller v. Kemp, 138 N.Y. 231, 33 N.E. 1034 (1893) (Discharges).

192. These provisions, enacted in 1936, now appear as §§ 5-1103–5-1109 of N.Y. General Obligations Law. The statutes require that, absent consideration, the offer, modification, or discharge be evidenced by a writing signed by the party against whom it is sought to be enforced.

193. See 19 Mich. Stats. Ann. (1970) § 26.987 (1) (Modifications and Discharges).

194. See U.C.C. § 2-205 (Firm Offers); § 2-209 (Modification, Rescission and Waiver).

195. The distinction is made explicit in § 89-B [§ 87] (Firm Offer) and § 89-D [§ 89] (Modification of Executory Contract) of *Restatement of Contracts (Second)*. Surprisingly, there seems to be no comparable treatment of discharges. Section 89-C [§ 88] deals with guaranties in much the same way that §§ 89-B [§ 87] and 89-D [§ 89] deal with firm offers and modifications.

196. See text at and following note 81 *supra*.

197. Sylvan Crest Sand & Gravel Co. v. United States, 150 F. 2d 642 (2d. Cir. 1945) is an excellent example.

198. See text following note 136 *supra*.

199. See particularly the discussion in 1A Corbin, Contracts § 152 *et seq.* (1936).

200. Among the best known are Adams v. Nichols, 19 Pick. 275 (Mass. 1837); School District No. 1 v. Dauchy, 25 Conn. 530 (1857); School Trustees of Trenton v. Bennett, 27 N.J.L. 513 (1859); Stees v. Leonard, 20 Minn. 494 (20 Gilfillan 448) (1874).

201. Text at note 103 *supra*.

202. The statement in the text is true with respect to the cases cited in note 200 *supra*. Since anything is possible, I would not be unduly surprised if someone could come up with a case of this type in which full "contractual" damages were awarded but I have never seen such a case.

203. Butterfield v. Byron, 153 Mass. 517, 27 N.E. 667 (1891)

became one of the leading cases. On the scope of the doctrine, see 6 Williston, Contracts § 1965 (rev. ed. 1938). (Professor Jaeger's edition of Williston has not, at the moment of writing, reached this point.)

204. As in Angus v. Scully, 176 Mass. 357, 57 N.E. 674 (1900), where a house, which was in process of being moved from its original location to a new one, was destroyed by fire after having been moved halfway.

205. In *Butterfield v. Byron*, note 203 *supra*, it appeared that the plaintiff (owner) was sueing in the interest of his insurance company, which had already reimbursed him for his loss. On the decline and fall of the rule which once permitted insurers to recover against third parties as assignees or subrogees of the insured's contract rights, see 2 Gilmore, Security Interests in Personal Property § 42.7.1 (1965).

206. Tarling v. Baxter, 6 B. & C. 360, 108 Eng. Rep. 484 (K.B. 1827) became the leading case. The rule was carried forward without change in both the English and the American codifications of sales law and currently appears as U.C.C. § 2-613.

207. For the cases see 1 Williston, Sales § 160 *et. seq.* (rev. ed. 1948).

208. Even when all the banks in the country were shut down, as during the "Banking Moratorium" of 1933, see Levy Plumbing Co. v. Standard Sanitary Mfg. Co., 68 S.W. 2d 273 (Tex. Civ. App. 1933).

209. Bowes v. Shand, L.R. 2 App. Ca. 455 (H.L. 1877); Norrington v. Wright, 115 U.S. 188 (1885); Filley v. Pope, 115 U.S. 213 (1885).

210. Honnold, *Buyer's Right of Rejection*, 97 U. Pa. L. Rev. 457 (1949) is an excellent discussion of the rule.

211. See, e.g., Mitsubishi Goshi Kaisha v. J. Aron, 16 F. 2d 185 (2d Cir. 1926) (per L. Hand, J.).

212. See U.C.C. §§ 2-504, 2-508, 2-601, 2-612.

213. Thus the destruction before delivery of specific goods contracted to be sold (text at note 206 *supra*) was a case of "objective" impossibility, wherefore seller was discharged; contrariwise, buyer's inability to pay (text at note 208 *supra*) was a case of "subjective" impossibility, wherefore buyer was not discharged. The *First Restatement of Contracts* accepted the distinction in § 455 (Subjective Impossibility Distinguished from Objective Impossibility).

214. The term seems to have come into use, first in England and then in this country, following the so-called Coronation cases of which Krell v. Henry, [1903] L.R. 2 K.B. 740 and Chandler v. Webster, [1904] L.R. 1 K.B. 493 are the best known. The procession and other festivities which were to have been held in connection with the coronation of Edward VII had to be called off at the last minute because of the King's sudden illness. In *Krell* the defendant had rented rooms from which to view the procession but was not under his agreement required to pay for them until (as it turned out) after the procession was canceled: *held* that he need not pay. *Chandler* was a similar case except that the payment was to be made before the cancellation was announced: *held* that the payment must be made. The decision in *Chandler* was much criticized and was eventually abrogated by statute in the Law Reform (Frustrated Contracts) Act of 1943 (6 & 7 Geo. 6 c.40).

215. *Krell v. Henry*, note 214 *supra*, illustrates the discharge of a paying party.

216. See the opinion or speech of Lord Atkin in Bell v. Lever Brothers, Inc., L.R. 1932 A.C. 161 (1931), where the suggestion that the two categories ("mistake" and "frustration") are identical was put forward for, so far as I know, the first time.

217. See, e.g., Berman, *Excuse for Nonperformance in the Light of Contract Practices in International Trade*, 63 Colum. L. Rev. 1413 (1963).

218. See the opinion of Traynor, J., in Lloyd v. Murphy, 25 Cal. 2d 48, 153 P. 2d 47 (1944).

219. Chapter 14 (§§ 454–69).

220. Section 288 (Frustration of the Object or Effect of the Contract). Illustration 1 codified *Krell v. Henry*, note 214 *supra*.

221. U.C.C. § 2-615 (Excuse by Failure of Presupposed Conditions).

222. See Van Hecke, *Changing Emphasis in Specific Performance*, 40 N.C. L. Rev. 1 (1961). A recent case of this type, with an exceptionally fine opinion by Judge Gasch, is City Stores Co. v. Ammerman, 266 F. Supp. 766 (D.D.C. 1967) *aff'd*, per curiam, 394 F. 2d 950 (D.C. Cir. 1968).

223. 11 Williston, Contracts §§ 1340, 1341, (3d ed. Jaeger 1968).

224. Comment, *Lost Profits as Contract Damages*, 65 Yale L. J. 992 (1956).

225. See Comment, *Once More into the Breach: Promissory Estoppel and Traditional Damage Doctrine*, 37 U. of Chi. Rev. 559, 588 *et. seq.* (1970).

226. On *Hadley* and the nineteenth century reaction, see Lecture 2, text beginning at note 113 to end of chapter. On the rejection of the assumption of risk idea, see U.C.C. § 2-715, Comment 2.

227. The Heron II (Kaufos v. C. Czarnikow, Ltd.) [1967] 3 All. E. L. R. 686.

IV. Conclusions and Speculations

228. It is an historical truism that assumpsit, from which our theories of contract eventually emerged, was itself a split-off from the tort action of trespass on the case. Until the late nineteenth century the dividing line between "contract" and "tort" had never been sharply drawn—see, e.g., the "great case" of *Coggs v. Bernard* (1702) and Holmes's elaborate demonstration in *The Common Law* that the "true explanation" of the great case was that it sounded not in contract but in tort (note 38 *supra*). No doubt the obscure realization that contract (or assumpsit) had its origins in tort accounted, at least in part, for the failure to make clear distinction between contract and tort until the nineteenth century theorists insisted on drawing the line.

229. On the restrictive theories of tort liability, as formulated by Holmes, see text at and following note 29 *supra*. A few examples of the expansiveness of twentieth-century tort theories will be presently commented on in the text.

230. See, generally, Lectures 1 and 2.

231. See, generally, Lecture 3.

232. Both the date and title of Keener, *Quasi-Contracts* (1893) are misleading. Keener himself was a thorough-going Langdellian: he went from Harvard to Columbia, where he became Dean of the Law School, carrying case-method teaching with him. The book, which represented an obsolete approach to the law even when it was written, looked much more to the past than to the future. Keener used the term "quasi-contract" in a narrow and technical sense, which had almost no point of contact with subsequent developments.

233. See text at note 180 *supra*.

234. *Restatement of Contracts (Second), Tentative Draft*

No. 2 165 (1965). The omissions in the passage quoted are cross-references to the Restatements of Agency, Torts, and Restitution.

235. See text at note 152 *supra*.

236. See text at note 173 *supra*.

237. Indeed Comment 2 to § 89A [§ 86] suggests, somewhat tentatively, that a Statute of Frauds defense would not (or might not) be available in an § 89A [§ 86] action. *Restatement of Contracts (Second), Tentative Draft No. 2*, 131–32 (1965).

238. 56 Cal. 2d. 583, 364 P. 2d 685, 15 Cal. Reptr. 821 (1961), *cert. denied* 368 U.S. 987 (1962).

239. 73 Cal. Reptr. 369, 447 P. 2d 609 (1968).

240. 74 Cal. Reptr. 225, 449 P. 2d 161 (1969).

241. Greenman v. Yuba Power Products, Inc., 59 Cal. 2d 57, 372 P. 2d 897, 27 Cal. Reptr. 697 (1962); Seely v. White Motor Co., 63 Cal. 2d 1, 403 P. 2d 145, 45 Cal. Reptr. 17 (1965).

242. In less than ten years an enormous literature about products liability has been piled up. One of the more interesting recent contributions is a symposium, *Products Liability: Economic Analysis and the Law*, 38 U. of Chi. L. Rev. 1 (1970). The principal article in the symposium, McKean, "Products Liability: Trends and Implications," is by an economist who takes a dim view of what has been going on in the law. Professor McKean's article is then discussed in commentaries prepared by several economic and legal hands (including myself). I need hardly make the point that I qualified for the symposium as a legal and not an economic hand.

243. The reporter for the *Restatement of Torts (Second)* was the late Dean William Prosser, who had effectively championed the § 402A approach. See his articles, *The Assault on the Citadel*

(*Strict Liability to the Consumer*), 69 Yale L.J. 1099 (1960); *The Fall of the Citadel* (*Strict Liability to the Consumer*), 50 Minn. L. Rev. 791 (1966). The course of development since 1940 is admirably traced in the successive editions of *Prosser on Torts*.

244. See the article by McKean in the Chicago symposium, note 242 *supra*. For a counter-argument, see my Commentary, 38 U. of Chi. L. Rev. 103 (1970).

245. For one example, consider the development, since the 1940s, of the idea that the liability of shipowners to their employees under the so-called doctrine of unseaworthiness is "a species of liability without fault . . . a form of absolute duty owing to all within the change of its humanitarian policy" (Rutledge, J., in Seas Shipping Co. v. Sieracki, 328 U.S. 85, 94–95 [1946]). This development is traced in Gilmore & Black, The Law of Admiralty § 6-38 *et. seq.* (1957).

246. See text at note 6 *supra*.

247. According to Posner, *A Theory of Negligence*, 1 J. of Legal Studies 29 (1972) there is an "orthodox view" (which Professor Posner does not share) of the attempt to restrict tort liability under the nineteenth century formulation of negligence theory (see, e.g., the Holmesian version discussed in the text at note 30 *supra*). The "orthodox" explanation attributed this development to, among other things, the "pressure of industrial expansion" and the "desire to subsidize the infant industries of the period." Professor Posner refers to Calabresi, *The Costs of Accidents, A Legal and Economic Analysis* (1970) and my own Commentary in the Chicago *Products Liability* symposium (note 242 *supra*) as exemplifying "various strands of the orthodox view" (*id.* at 30, note 1). Wherever the truth may lie, the idea of the close relationship between nineteenth century legal theory and nineteenth century economic theory, which seemed novel when Professor Friedman advanced it in 1965, is becoming a commonplace.

For other examples, see note 7 *supra*. Professor Posner feels that nineteenth century negligence theory was economically as well as legally sound and that the gradual erosion of the theory in this century is to be deplored. If he turns his attention to contract, his conclusions will no doubt be the same.

248. Thus Story, in an "Address on the Progress of Jurisprudence" delivered to the Suffolk Bar in 1821: "The mass of the law is . . . accumulating with an almost incredible rapidity. . . . It is impossible not to look without some discouragement upon the ponderous volumes which the next half century will add to the groaning shelves of our jurists." He went on to suggest that some kind of codification was the "one adequate remedy" which might "avert the fearful calamity, which threatens us, of being buried alive, not in the catacombs, but in the labyrinths of the law." J. Story, Miscellaneous Writings 198, 237 (ed. W. W. Story 1852).

249. See the proposal submitted by Story to the governor of Massachusetts in 1837, text at note 11 *supra*.

250. I have traced this story in *Commercial Law in the United States: Its Codification and Other Misadventures*, which appears in Aspects of Comparative Commercial Law 449 (ed. Ziegel and Foster 1969). This was an after-dinner speech delivered at a banquet held in connection with a Conference at McGill University, September, 1968; the speech is reprinted as it was given, without footnotes or supporting documentation.

251. 41 U.S. (16 Pet.) 1 (1842).

252. One example of how this process worked, at its best, is the series of Supreme Court cases, from the 1860s through the 1880s, which determined the validity of after-acquired property clauses as well as the priority for purchase money advances in the context of railroad and industrial financing. See 1 Gilmore, Security Interests in Personal Property § 2.4 (1965); 2 *id.* §§ 28.1–28.3.

253. Although it has not proved to be as easy to do away with the idea of the general federal commercial law as Justice Brandeis may have assumed when he wrote the opinion for the Court in Erie R.R. v. Tompkins, 304 U.S. 64 (1938). See Friendly, *In Praise of Erie—and of the New Federal Common Law,* 39 N.Y.U. L. Rev. 383 (1964).

254. On the purification of doctrine, see text at the beginning of Lecture 3.

255. On Langdell's ideas, see text following note 20 *supra*.

256. I do not mean to suggest that Holmes was doctrinaire in the same sense that Langdell was. Holmes kept his own theories open-ended by his reiterated insistence that law basically reflects social and economic conditions and must change as they change. However, Williston's documentation of Holmes's insights was carried out in what we might call a thoroughly Langdellian spirit.

257. See text at beginning of Lecture 2.

258. Just as the New York Court of Appeals, under the influence of Cardozo's broad and vague theory of consideration (see text at and following note 136 *supra*), never had to resort to promissory estoppel. In this connection, see particularly Cardozo's opinion in the *Allegheny College* case (note 141 *supra*) in which he plays with promissory estoppel on his way to the conclusion that "without recourse to the innovation of promissory estoppel the transaction can be fitted within the mould of consideration as established by tradition."

Since the 1940s the American innovation, usually described as "equitable estoppel," has made some progress in England. See the opinion of Lord Denning in Central London Property Trust, Ltd. v. High Trees House, Ltd. [1947] K.B. 130; Combe v. Combe, [1951] 2 K.B. 215. The latter case is frequently cited to the proposition that "equitable estoppel" is a "shield and not a sword"—that is, it can be pleaded by way of defense but cannot be used as an affirmative ground of recovery. See Atiyah, An Introduction to the Law of Contract 86 *et seq.* (2d ed. 1971), Kessler & Gilmore, Contracts—Cases and Materials (1970) collects some of the recent English literature in a Note at p. 498.

259. Text at note 142 *supra.*

Bibliography

Selected book reviews and extended discussions of *The Death of Contract,* mostly from law reviews.

Adams, John. Book Review. 1975 Wash. U. L.Q. 858.

Braucher, Jean. *The Afterlife of Contract.* 90 NW U. L. Rev. (1995).

Braucher, Robert. *Contracts.* In *American Law: The Third Century* 121 (Bernard Schwartz, ed., 1976).

Collins, Ronald K. L. *Gilmore's Grant (or the Life and Afterlife of Grant Gilmore and His Death).* 90 NW U. L. Rev. (1995).

Dalton, Clare. Book Review. 24 Am. U. L. Rev. 1372 (1975).

Danzig, Richard. *The Death of Contract and the Life of the Profession: Observations on the Intellectual State of Legal Academia.* 29 Stan. L. Rev. 1125 (1977).

Epstein, Richard. Book Review. 20 Am. J. Legal Hist. 68 (1976).

Farber, Daniel. *The Ages of American Formalism.* 90 NW U. L. Rev. (1995).

Farnsworth, E. Allan. *"Contracts Is Not Dead."* 77 Cornell L. Rev. 1034 (1992).

Feinman, Jay M. *The Significance of Contract Theory.* 58 U. Cin. L. Rev. 1283, 1289–94 (1990).

Gordley, James R. Book Review. 89 Harv. L. Rev. 452 (1975).

Gordon, Robert. Book Review. 1974 Wis. L. Rev. 1216 (1975).

Hillman, Robert. *The Triumph of Gilmore's* The Death of Contract. 90 NW U. L. Rev. (1995).

―――. *The Crisis in Modern Contract Theory.* 67 Tex. L. Rev. 103, 113–18 (1988).

Holmes, Eric M. *Is There Life after Gilmore's* Death of Contract? *Inductions from a Study of Commercial Good Faith in First Party Insurance Contracts.* 65 Cornell L. Rev. 330 (1980).

Horwitz, Morton J. Book Review. 42 U. Chi. L. Rev. 787 (1975).

Kastely, Amy. *Cogs or Cyborgs? Blasphemy and Irony in Contract Theories.* 90 NW U. L. Rev. (1995).

Kaufman, Colin. *The Resurrection of Contract.* 17 Washburn L.J. 38 (1977).

Linzer, Peter. *The Decline of Assent.* 20 Ga. L. Rev. 323 (1986).

―――. *Law's Unity: An Essay for the Master Contortionist.* 90 NW U. L. Rev. (1995).

Macintosh, Kerry L. *Gilmore Spoke Too Soon: Contract Rises from the Ashes of the Bad Faith Tort.* 27 Loy. L.A. L. Rev. 483 (1994).

Milhollin, Gary L. *More on* The Death of Contract. 24 Cath. U. L. Rev. 29 (1975).

Milsom, S. F. C. *A Pageant in Modern Dress.* 84 Yale L.J. 1585 (1975).

Mooney, Ralph James. *The Rise and Fall of Classical Contract: A Response to Professor Gilmore.* 55 Ore. L. Rev. 155 (1976).

O'Connell, Jeffrey, and Thomas O'Connell. "Holmes & Gilmore." In Book Review. 67 Notre Dame L. Rev. 167, 180–82 (appendix) (1991).

Patterson, Dennis. *Langdell's Legacy.* 90 NW U. L. Rev. (1995).

Peters, Ellen. The Death of Contract: *Foreword.* 90 NW U. L. Rev. (1995).

Reitz, John. Book Review. 123 U. Pa. L. Rev. 697 (1975).

Rubin, Edward. *The Non-Judicial Life of Contract: Beyond the Shadow of the Law.* 90 NW U. L. Rev. (1995).

Speidel, Richard. *An Essay on the Reported Death and Continued Vitality of Contract.* 27 Stan. L. Rev. 1161 (1975).

———. *Afterword: The Shifting Domain of Contract.* 90 NW U. L. Rev. (1995).

Sullivan, Timothy. Book Review. 17 Wm. & Mary L. Rev. 403 (1975).

Testy, Kellye. *An Unlikely Resurrection.* 90 NW U. L. Rev. (1995).

Von Mehren, Arthur T. Book Review. 75 Colum. L. Rev. 1404 (1974).

Waters, Anthony Jon. Book Review. 36 Md. L. Rev. 270 (1976).

———. *For Grant Gilmore.* 42 Md. L. Rev. 865 (1983).

Wessman, Mark B. *Should We Fire the Gatekeeper? An Examination of the Doctrine of Consideration.* 48 U. Miami L. Rev. 45–49 (1993).

Yablon, Charles. *Grant Gilmore, Holmes, and the Anxiety of Influence.* 90 NW U. L. Rev. (1995).

Table of Cases

173

Index

175